MW01235238

THROUGH
THE FLAMES TO THE CROSS

THROUGH
THE FLAMES TO THE CROSS
One Man's journey to the fullness of God's grace

EUGENE TOMLINSON

XULON PRESS

Xulon Press
2301 Lucien Way #415
Maitland, FL 32751
407.339.4217
www.xulonpress.com

© 2018 by Eugene Tomlinson

All rights reserved solely by the author. The author guarantees all contents are original and do not infringe upon the legal rights of any other person or work. No part of this book may be reproduced in any form without the permission of the author. The views expressed in this book are not necessarily those of the publisher.

Unless otherwise indicated, Scripture quotations taken from the Holy Bible, New International Version (NIV). Copyright © 1973, 1978, 1984, 2011 by Biblica, Inc.™. Used by permission. All rights reserved.

Printed in the United States of America.

ISBN-13: 978-1-54562-199-8

FOREWORD

I have been a pastor of a local church for most of my adult life. As a pastor, I have the opportunity to know and walk with many people through life. Gene Tomlinson is one of those people I have been so encouraged to know and watch grow. Gene has always been a "treasure seeker." Not, of mere financial treasure but always looking for the next and greatest adventure that brings life its richest meaning. From his early days of making Jesus Christ Lord of his life, to the more recent days of pastoring back in his own hometown of Southport, Gene has always been one of those guys who did all that he did in life with all of his energy and focus. In my opinion, this is what made Gene a "treasure seeker."

I suppose I always felt a certain affinity toward Gene because we had so much in common. We both loved to go for it in life, to take risks, to live life with all of our might. We both loved the out-doors too; hunting, fishing, boating and the like. We both enjoy cooking. Mostly because we both love to eat!

We love to create and experiment with taste, texture and spices—creating that special dish that is just amazing! More than anything else, I love to watch people like Gene discover that while he is just an ordinary "container," he is a "container" in whom the greatest treasure of all now fully dwells.It is this reality that sets Gene apart from others around him. He knows that everything he is and every-thing he does, is because of the life of another who lives His life in Gene. Gene is just one of the ordinary guys who has stumbled upon this "mystery" that has been "hidden from ages and genera-tions past, but is now made known to the saints, which is, Christ in you the hope of Glory" (Col. 1:27-28).

Gene realizes that he has this treasure in earthen vessels and now all that he is, is but a reflection of the God that lives His life in Gene. Therefore, Gene is no longer a mere treasure seeker, but one who possesses the greatest treasure of all. God Himself is the treasure in Gene's life. It is Gene's desire to share that treasure with you now: Gene, the ordinary container—God the extraordinary treasure! Real people, ordinary in every respect, but inhabited by the God that has created and holds everything together by his very presence. Yet He is willing to live His life in us, through us and even as us!

Pastor Steve Mattis
Wilmington, North Carolina

CHAPTER ONE

L et's take a bit of a journey in time. Living through the seventies with a sex, drugs, rock-n-roll mentality quickly changes from a turn on, tune in "drop out 'lifestyle. Was coming to a quick change. Here come the eighties, and the "where is the party", the get up, put on your boogie shoes and dance the night away mentality.

Going from a baby boomer that was against war, inequality, the system, anything that represented authority, to big hair, tight -fitting clothes, bright lights and disco. This was a totally new type of drug- fueled lifestyle. The Stones, Credence Clear Water, Santana, Hendrix, Morrison, Pink Floyd were fading. New names and new music brought in the Disco era: Donna Summer, Michael Jackson, Bee Gees, Village People, Kool and the Gang, Barry White were our new chart toppers.

New clubs with bright lights and big dance floors replaced house parties with black lights and quadraphonic eight track stereos. There were new drugs that produced higher levels of energy to perform all the new high energy dance moves. This was a period of time where everything was changing. Gone were the peace loving and Woodstock era hippies wearing patched up bell bottom jeans and dessert boots. Now it was all about that look, big collars, flowing sleeve shirts, miniskirts with patent leather boots. Pretty much the antithesis of the look of the 1960's and 1970's.

This chapter is a look at my life during those times – a very dark season in my life.

Waking up in the morning during the early 80's was pretty much the same most days. Whew! What a night last night was! All the necessary ingredients: live music, dancing, partying, partying supplies, catching a primo buzz and partying to the wee hours of the morning. Now is the hardest part of the day, getting up and getting going for a busy day on the beach. Being the operator of a beach service business on a busy South Carolina resort was not a job that many would consider as a demanding job. My day started before 9am by setting out the chairs and umbrellas, followed by rigging the Aqua Cats and Hobie Cats and Windsurfers for a full day of rentals and lessons. One of the tougher tasks of the day was to choose the most perfect spot to hangout to maintain a well-tanned beach guy look.

As the guest began to arrive for a day on the beach, many would joke with us about how tough our job must be. Yep, it was a tough way to live: surfing, windsurfing and sailing our days away. Our fun was often interrupted by a call for help, amazingly, those female cries of distress got much quicker attention. For a bunch of twenty something year old guys, I guess this was just natural. We did have a couple of girls on staff as well. These girls knew us and in that knowledge, were not interested in us outside of work. We all seemed connected by a common interest, summer fun. It seemed like our focus was fixed on all that was immediately in front of us. The thought of long term vision never really had a chance to influence our thoughts or plans. We lived totally in the moment, whether flying a hull on a Hobie, catching some air windsurfing or carving up a nice clean wave surfing.

As our days started winding down, the topics of our conversations turned to making our party plans for the evening. We put away the chairs and umbrellas, windsurfers and sail boats remembering the highs associated with a great day on the beach. Our motto was appropriately, "a bad day on the beach was much better than a good day doing anything else". My ride home was about thirty minutes, a great break to catch my breath and get ready for my evening routine: a five-mile jog, sit-ups, pushups and jumping jacks. A very simple routine, but necessary to keep that well-conditioned look running around in surfing shorts all day, every day.

The unknown to many I interacted with was the darkness of the life I lived after my shower and a light dinner. A habit that started innocently enough ten years earlier had grown into a full-blown addiction to cocaine. What started as smoking pot and dealing drugs had now become my other life. It would consume the next seven to eight hours each night. Drinking and whichever was the most available mood enhancer took over.

The other area of responsibility in my day was making sure all my friends/customers had what was required for them to party in the manner they chose. The dealing was an important supplement to my income as well. These finances were necessary to support the drug- fueled lifestyle I was living. Through the years most drug dealers understand the loyalty of many friends is based on how well you keep them supplied.

Many evenings when customers came by, they would sample the drugs, and the party would be on. I can't say I remember much of those parties much less names of those attending. We did party hard, smoking dope, doing MDA, Acid/LSD, THC, Coke, you name it, we did it. When our levels of stimulation maxed out, we turned to barbiturates of many sorts to bring us down. This was referred to as" roller -coasting", up then down. It is by the grace of God only that many of us lived through these days.

One of these friends I was supplying wanted to introduce me to a new and better way of doing cocaine. This involved a dangerous process of separating pure cocaine from the cut and them smoking only pure cocaine. When I inhaled the first hit, euphoria set in, in about thirty seconds. My second hit was about twenty minutes later- I was flying. Then in about ten minutes I took a third hit, this made me sick, immediately afterwards, I was sailing away. Your body tries to reject drugs that pure; too bad I didn't get the message. The effect was short lived, thus about every twenty minutes came the need for more. The troubling part was, none of the following hits produced highs that would satisfy, there was always a longing for more. The high would lead to the feeling of being wired, agitated and frustrated. My body would beg to come down and sleep. That was a very rough state to be in, very restless, short tempered and a good sleep hard to achieve. This was no fun! I became obsessive, compulsive and mainly in denial. I was addicted. The fun loving, party guy who had it" made in the shade" had truly become "Mean Gene".

After five or six hours of tossing and turning sleep, it was time to go back to the beach. A good joint was usually a great remedy to a day that started out feeling kind of rough. Getting out to the beach and taking a quick dip was usually good for washing out the cobwebs as well. The daily routine and the various activities of the day usually cleared me up and had me prepared for another night of partying.

I began to plan many of my activities around the internal craving to stimulate my body. There were many days, my new best friend, the pipe, would beckon me and the countdown of minutes till I could once again be high started. No matter how much fun I thought I was having, a very sad reality dawned on me. The numbers of people in my life, the women, the parties had become a blur to me. Sadly, most of these events I could never remember. There were never enough drugs, money, women or parties, to fill the hole in my soul. Life had become very repetitious, dissatisfying, nothing was any longer relevant.

The great thing about living in the Low Country of South Carolina was that beach weather could start as early as mid-March and run through November. The seasonal nature of the weather with the demands of the beach services made trips to Florida, and the Caribbean Islands to keep fresh supply of drugs possible. These trips usually took several days, primarily so not to raise suspicion that quick trips would. Upon arrival, I would hang out with the guys that I was doing business with. For a couple of days, we would eat, drink and make merry, sampling the newest in their lines of party favors. During these days, we could also tell if there were any unwanted eyes on us. When it came the day to do the deal it was business, all business. We all carried guns for the protection of the deal, making sure those the drugs were intended for ended up leaving with the drugs and those that the money belonged to ended up leaving with the money. These trips were always different, sometimes by boat, others by car and still others by plane. On our return trips there was never any use of drugs. We felt it was necessary to be aware at all times of everything going on around us that could hinder our return or cause us loss on any level.

During this season of my life, the relationship with my family was very strained. There was also no evidence in my life of any type of relationship with God. I am a name sake; thus, my father and I share the same name. During these years sadly, the similarities ended there. He was a very Godly man of the highest morals and integrity in all his dealings. My guess is that I inherited my love of the water and sailing from him. He shared with me that on a visit to Rose Island in the Bahamas, that after docking and registering in the marina, a couple of locals who recognized the name on the marina registry approached the boat to see if there was anything they could get him. He and mom were overwhelmed by their friendly nature, not quite sure they knew what they were being offered. Some years later it dawned on my parents these guys may not have been the nice guys they originally thought them to be, they realized the guys thought, by the name, it was me and wanted to sell some drugs. My family was aware of very many of my life's activities, they had never been confronted with it in this manner.

In the eighties with the onset of the disco, the popularity and demand for cocaine increased dramatically. As this demand increased, there were many that pursued the ability to make the very lucrative money that came with it. Many cartels from the Caribbean Islands, Jamaica, South America, and Mexico formed associations in areas where they felt it would be profitable and easy to move into and set up dealing operations. Since neither I nor anyone I dealt with was with a larger group, the Low Country was open for a more organized group to take over. These takeovers happened in several ways. They used scare tactics against me which included breaking into my home twice, late night threatening phone calls, and a failed attempt to fire bomb my house. I was not able to go to the police as I did not want the attention from them, especially since they already knew me. I will speak more of this in chapter 5.

Moving to South Carolina was meant to be a new, fresh start in life. What it turned into was an ever-increasing downward spiral. After living nearly eight years of a drug infused lifestyle, the consequences started to become much more than I had ever expected.

During mid-summer 1986, after a drug and alcohol fueled night of partying, I made a very bad decision to try to impress a couple of ladies with a midnight Hobie sail. After rigging the boat, I hoisted the sail, the wind was coming out of the only direction possible to fill the sail. I don't remember ever seeing a boat set sail that quickly.

Regretfully, as the boat raced into the darkness, it was not manned. That is the last time the boat was ever seen. The next morning as I went in to work, I was surprised as everyone else that one of our boats was missing. I filed a police report for a stolen Hobie Cat. As this was investigated, the security guards at the front gate reported my late-night visit to the police, and just that quickly I was released from my beach service obligations.

In my state of mind, I welcomed the extra time to deal and feed my out of control addiction. The police attention towards me increased as did other unwanted attention. To escape all these issues, I tried to numb myself to the reality of life with the pipe which was always ready to be filled with free base. One evening after a friend and I had been drugging for about ten hours, I looked at my stash, enough for a month of heavy use and became paranoid that I was running out. In a very angry and agitated state I went in the bathroom and looked in the mirror, I did not like what I saw.. Upon coming out of the bathroom, I realized the person that had been there had left and left a note that questioned my sanity to the highest degree.

Angrily I turned to my best friend, the pipe. I started filling it to levels I had never done and was not getting any higher. There was no escape for where I was. Still with plenty of coke I called a friend of mine at 4:30am asking for more. He angrily said to me "Man you have lost it, never call me again". At this point anger really took over, the pipe had betrayed me. I went to the bathroom again to throw some water on my face and there staring at me out of the mirror was this guy that I didn't recognize; he was angry, paranoid, twisted, tormented, not any fun for anyone or myself. It was in fact the darkest, ugliest realization of my life. I went back, shattered the pipe, poured out my processing liquid and never smoked free base cocaine again. After so much bad had gone on during this season in my life, there was one night that revealed to me exactly what I had gotten into. I was called to make a delivery in downtown Charleston. It did not dawn on me that I was being set up. Yes, it was a very violent time and there were many wanting me out of the picture.

I put the delivery together and took the short ride to the house where the exchange was to take place. After a few words, the folks had what they had ordered, I had the money and was out the door. There were two guys hanging out on the side walk, as I went to walk by them, one of them bumped into me, when I went to push him off, he spun me around. The other man had a gun aimed directly in my face. They ordered me down an alley close to the house, cracked me over the back of the head with the pistol. While I was on the ground, they took the money from me. They were after more than the money. As I was in a semi-conscious state, the man placed the gun behind my ear and pulled the trigger, the gun did not fire and he pulled the trigger again. The gun did not fire the second time either. At this time, I began to get my wits back about me and came to very angry. As I got up, the two men fled down the street and out of sight very quickly. As I lost sight of them, I heard a voice speak to me, "I know the plans I have for you." I was not in a place to realize this was God speaking to me or that He had in fact delivered me from the murderous plans the men had for me. My pride took a tremendous shot that night. It was time for me to realize what a dark and dangerous life I was living. My initial reaction was to do what I had gotten used to doing when things went bad, run. Later in life, I learned that was in fact the Lord speaking to me that night and that I could only run from God and His plans for me for so long. There were beginning to be very few safe places for me to run now.

I moved back home, to Southport, the end of the summer 1986. The reflection of the guy in the mirror I saw scared me. In retrospect, what caused the greatest fear to me was the reality of an eternity in the flames – separated forever from the cross.

CHAPTER 2
GROWING UP IN A SMALL SOUTHERN TOWN IN THE 60'S.

THE FORMATIVE YEARS

While looking back at life with the realization of what an interesting trip it has been, I formulate thoughts and memories that will hopefully allow you to have a glimpse that leads to a understanding as to who I am, where I come from and the influences that led to me being me. Hopefully this will spur some to connect in some respect with the experiences and memories that mold us into who we become.

As far back as my memory serves me, Southport, North Carolina has been my home. I was born in the spring of 1954 in a small hospital serving the community and Brunswick County. Later that year a very significant event occurred that has stayed in the minds of most folks living on the south-east coast of America, Hurricane Hazel. This was a very powerful storm that brought wide spread damage and destruction to the Cape Fear region. At the time, I was only 6 months old and don't really remember it. One assurance I can pass along – it wasn't my fault.

My parents, Eugene B Tomlinson and Atha Leigh Wallace were both born in Fayetteville, NC. Their families both enjoyed spending times on Long Beach, NC. These times at the beach on summer vacation led to a romance that became a marriage and then a family. My guess is the DNA passed on to me by both my parents included the deep love I have for this area. Dad graduated from the U.S. Naval Academy followed by serving his commitment to our country in the Navy. Mom lost her mother at a very young age and helped her Dad, Watson Wallace, raise a younger brother and two younger sisters. Mom and Dad's love of this area brought them here to live and start a family. Mom and Dad started a TV shop and laundromat which got them settled here. During this time, the U.S. Government built Sunny Point Ocean Military Terminal which was on the Cape Fear River with close access to the Atlantic Ocean. Dad was hired and placed in charge of military traffic in logistics. Sunny Point has grown to be the largest ammunition shipping depot on the East Coast of America. Being a man of many ambitions, Dad also became the Mayor of Southport, a position he ultimately filled for 22 years.

Mom was the perfect picture of a wife and mother during these years. There were very few spare moments in Mom's day. There were five children in our family and we were always greeted with a great breakfast the most important meal of the day, brown paper bag lunches, clean pressed clothes and sent off on our ten to fifteen-minute walk to school with a prayer to behave and have a great day.

The walk to school was so very special in our town, not sure any of us fully realized the utopia we lived in. As we would walk with the other children from our neighborhood, our walk took us past the Cape Fear River, streets lined with long leaf pines and majestic live oaks that formed a canopy over many 100 to 150-year-old homes. Maybe the beautiful setting of blooming azaleas, dogwoods and honeysuckle escaped us then, remembering those fragrances with birds chirping and squirrels playing seems like almost yesterday.

Those walks included much fun and laughter, sometimes hurt feelings or a bumped knee produced a very quick passing tear. Stopping to play in the gentleman pirate, Stede Bonnet's, creek often sent us home wet and muddy and full of tales to tell. Thinking back, there were no less than ten families and most had at least three children, five or six children was normal. We were encouraged to refer to the others as children, as kids were baby goats. I guess many of us made the mistake of saying things or doing things that weren't the desired behavior and learned very quickly soap did not taste good nor did switches feel good. Many points were made and taken in that manner.

Southport was a segregated city during this time, not really sure if any of us really understood it and there wasn't much talk about it. That is just how it was and to us just how it had always been, no disrespect was added. As we went to school it was the Caucasian children in one school and the Negro children in another. The simplistic lifestyle in our town never really led us to question the separation. In hind sight, we never really had the benefit of the relationships we could have had.

Southport High School was the home of the Dolphins, this school was built in 1922 and unfortunately burned down in January 1969, arson was the cause. This school housed all twelve grades and was very well loved by all who attended. There were some very colorful personalities that added to a great experience there.

We had baseball, basketball and football there which created a very high level of community excitement during whichever season it was. Many of my early childhood heroes were the larger than life guys who played these sports while being cheered on by the most beautiful girls in the world that just happened to be our JV and Varsity cheerleaders.

Southport was a very church oriented town as well. Most of the buildings were old, with beautiful architecture and housed the Baptist, Methodist, Episcopal, Catholic, Presbyterian and Apostolic congregations. As children, we really didn't know the difference except that if you were invited to dinner on Friday with Catholics – you ate fish, growing up in a seaside community, we loved fish. Many days you would hear church music or chimes ringing out all over town from the different churches bell towers. One of the first responsibilities I had at church was to play church music on Sunday mornings before church. I think every child had that one child as a friend, you know a little Johnny, the one you were most prone to get in trouble with – I did. For my fourteenth birthday, my parents gave me a record player, the flip top type that played 33's and 45's. My parents felt the best value was albums, as you got more songs. For my first album, Mom and Dad gave me "Born to be Wild" by Steppenwolf. I really loved that album which pleased Mom and

Dad. Little Johnny really liked that album, so we mutually decided it was our obligation to share it with downtown Southport. The following Sunday morning we played it from our church loud speaker, and it worked, many residents heard it well as our pastor! Needless to say, I didn't have to worry about showing up for church early anymore – so much for an early attempt at turning the church contemporary. My dad was of course concerned by this behavior and spent quality time of correction with me. After a few days of carefully sitting on the softest of chairs, I began what seemed to be an eternity of pulling weeds from the garden, a couple of weeks of restriction, especially cutting into the time little Johnny and I could be an influence on each other – I realized the errors of my ways.

When Southport High School burned down in 1969, it led to many changes in our town. The Baptist Church and Methodist Church were close by and for convenience the classrooms in these churches became our school.

There has always been much speculation as to who burned the school – I can assure you I did not, nor did I know for sure for a very long time. What did increase speculation was shortly after the school burnt, there was a bomb threat on Southport Baptist Church. A couple of mornings later my friend approached me about having seen a very suspicious person leaving the back of the church. At fifteen I was very gullible and followed him to the basement of the church on a bomb search. It only took him a couple of minutes to find a clear plastic case with some batteries and test tubes in it which he said was a bomb, I was told to clear the way as he was bringing it out. The police station was right next door and much attention was paid to this heroic deed. This case was set on the sidewalk outside of the police station as he went inside to inform them of his find. By now, there were about 100 onlookers getting as close a look as possible, along comes a gust of wind and blows this thing over. Needless to say, the crowd cleared very quickly. Without much talking about this, my friend got to attend Carolina Military Academy for the rest of his high school years.

Life in Southport was always fun, so many of our activities were neighborhood based. As we walked home from school, plans were put in place for our baseball, basketball or football games. There were so many of us, we always had plenty for two teams. When it came time to choose teams, we had new best friends and those who were captains did the choosing. Each one of us had the desire to be chosen first and never being chosen last – this identity sure wasn't an ego booster. Being tackled in sand spurs or getting in cactus plants were not pleasurable experiences either and many times led to black eyes and words less that complimentary were exchanged. These actions generally led to being told on, more exposure to the bar of soap treatment or sitting gingerly for a few days.

We always appreciated our parents showing us their trust, many times this included looking after our younger siblings. (Oh joy) I had a younger sister and two younger brothers. A sure fired way to look after them was to help them up a tree. We had several large live oaks in our yard which made this approach to babysitting possible. I am not sure the younger ones really would agree as generally when they wanted to come down, there was no one there to help – thus they resigned themselves to staying in the tree. Not to worry though my parents had good ears and could identify each child by the sound of their sobs. After a few minutes of looking the children were located safe and sound up in the trees, right where we left them. That approach to babysitting was short lived.

Our justification for this type of behavior was to be on the river exploring. The Cape Fear was 300 yards away and the potential for adventure was much greater there. We fished, crabbed, clammed and hunted for all types of treasures on the shore, in the mud and swamp grass.

Our neighbor across the street was Captain John, one of the most wonderful men and man of the seas a child could ever know. He was the first to teach me about fishing, tying the knots, proper

tackle, bait, tides to fish on, and most importantly how to hold your mouth. He was there coaching me, as I caught my first croaker, spot, blowfish and the most prized flounder at 6 years old.

Crabbing was a bit different experience, you needed a chicken neck, a string, a sinker, a net and a good sense of feel. The art was sensing the tug and slowly pulling the crab up so not to lose it, then slipping the net under them to secure the catch. Captain John watched interestingly at my first attempt to remove the crab from the net, after a couple of painful lessons doing it my way, I was ready to listen to him, even to today, his method works the best.

I always wondered why no one taught us to clam on the river. My friend Robbie and I decided that by doing it would be the best way to learn. Armed with a couple of short tonged rakes and a bucket, we lit out for the river. In no time, we had covered ourselves from head to toe with mud and very quickly filled a five-gallon bucket with clams. Mom and Dad were out of town buying antiques for the shop we had, and our friend Ms. Underwood was looking after us. We very proudly presented her with our clams as our first choice for dinner. We went outside to rinse off all the thick, smelly, yet wonderfully achieved Cape Fear mud while she prepared our feast. Pride overwhelmed Robbie and me as we watched the other siblings and Ms. Underwood enjoying our catch. Dinner was interrupted by the phone ringing, it was Mom and Dad checking in for the day. Ms. Underwood very excitedly shared of our successful trip to the river and our enjoying the fruits of our labor -clams, there was silence for a moment, her response was, yes, across the street at the river. Her excitement and pleasure immediately faded. The clams were removed from the table and all of us encouraged to spit out what we had not swallowed. Robbie and I failed to read the signs posted about every 50 or so yards that stated "no shell fishing in the area due to contaminated water". Well, the water looked quite fine. Maybe there was something about those clams I could use to justify later in life behavior – if only.

The summers growing up were always the best. The beaches were close by, trips to visit my grandmother, Mama Mary in Lumberton, weeks at the North Carolina Baptist Assembly at Fort Caswell, Little League Baseball and yes, those pesky chores, mowing and weeding the yard to earn allowance. Very early in life I realized the strong love I had for the ocean and water related activities. Growing up we would spend many family times at the beach. We had so much fun, playing, swimming, building sandcastles and skim boarding. The days were just never long enough. Dad kept a boat and many Saturday and Sunday afternoons were spent water skiing down the Inter Coastal Waterway to local favorite spot – Yellow Banks. These times were my priorities until in the mid 60's when I was introduced to surfing. Very quickly that was all that mattered. Dad got me my first surfboard in 1968, a 7'9" Velzy. At the time people thought it to be way too short; two years later the surfing revolution quickly took over and most boards were a good 2 feet shorter.

During the summer while young we would visit Mama Mary, a fine Presbyterian, for a couple of weeks at a time. She was a very strong Christian lady and a firm believer in "spare the rod, spoil the child'. My going there was generally planned around Godwin Heights Baptist Church Vacation Bible School. It was Mama Mary's ambition that one of her "Baptist born, Baptist bred when I die, there will be a Baptist dead" grandchildren win the pin for being able to quote the most Bible verses from memory. I made her happy several times.

My grandfather passed when I was very young, and Mama Mary had never learned to drive. Saturday mornings after breakfast, with her top hat and purse over her arm, off to town we would march for the day, this was about a 30 minute very fast paced walk. This visit included a movie, admission was 6 coke bottle caps and 50¢ would pay for 3 drinks and popcorn. After the movie, we shopped at the Piggly Wiggly and repeated a very quick pace home. Her cooking was the best. I will never forget the club sandwiches she made, the cookies, cakes and ice cream were not bad either. She spoiled us as only a grandmother could. Yep – I did get into mischief there at times; her favorite form of correction was a quick application of a ruler to an open palm. There have been times in life I wish she were here to do it again.

The North Carolina Baptist Assembly was a short 20-minute ride away. This property was an old U.S. Army and Civil War Fort. The original fort was completed in 1836 and named after early N.C. Governor Richard Caswell. When North Carolina seceded from the Union, the Confederate Army made it along with the fort at Fort

Fisher, one of the most elaborate defense systems in the world at the time. With the old barracks converted to housing, plenty of bunkers to explore, a dining hall, recreation building, gymnasium, swimming pools, ocean front activities and the hangout, the Drift Inn; what more could a kid want? The days filled with activities Christian classes and good clean fun. What was good about these times was being able to meet people (girls) from all over the state. Some of these folks are still lifelong friends and others I have never forgotten.

In 1969 I was able to work on the staff. My job was being responsible for the gym and rec-room. I earned a whopping $15.00 a week plus room and board. I was the only staff person with a surfboard and boy was it a chic magnet, I loved that attention! Fort Caswell has always been and always will be one of my favorite places full of fond memories.

Easter weekend is generally when we start gearing up for summer here. Mom and Dad always made sure it was special. For as long as I can remember Mom made us Easter baskets, good Easter baskets. Easter Egg hunts have always been a highlight of our Easter weekends, a year would not pass without one. This tradition she carried forward for her grandchildren as well. Many Sundays during these years, right after church our parents would load us up in our 61 Chevy Wagon for a Sunday afternoon out. Our first stop on the trip would be at Beck's Seafood in Calabash for a fried seafood lunch. Our family was a family of 6 at this time and we could all eat plenty of fried flounder, shrimp, oysters and deviled crab, French fries, coleslaw, and hushpuppies for $12.00.

After lunch, we would continue south to Myrtle Beach, The Pavilion, Amusement Park and the rides. The sights and sounds, so much laughter filled the air, warm breezes off the ocean, the cars, the Beach music, made popular in this era – WOW! Dad's favorite and I must admit mine as well, The Calliope. We would finish the day with a hot dog from Peaches Corner – the memory leaves me speechless.

The highlight of summer was then as is still now, The N.C. Fourth of July Festival. This festival originated over 200 years ago and has grown every year since. All the activities, exhibitions, street dances, market in the park, parade, fireworks and so much more allowed us all to witness the Spirit of America, our independence and the message of patriotism. This is a 4-day festival that has grown in popularity over the years to where now our small hometown is rated as one of the top 10 places in America to spend the 4th of July.

All of these events and activities in a small-town environment contributed to my formative years. In this town, everyone knew everyone, and every parent was a surrogate parent to whoever was playing in their yard on any given day. Many days upon arriving home from afternoons of frolicking and play, I would have some "splaining" to do as news of my exploits, whether good or bad had already reached my parents. Some days included discipline. This discipline made it important to stay in good relationship with my brothers or sisters as Mom would assign them the task of going to the bush in the backyard to pick the switch - a rather dubious honor.

Growing up in Southport was a real blessing. Family was at the core of all we did. We went to church as a family, went out as a family, we grew up as a family. My parents raised us with a constant message of God, love, family, education, community, country in that order as the core of who we are.

Yep, we made bad choices, had friends that made bad choices and as friends we helped each other make bad choices.

Looking back in my formative years, listening to and being obedient to those older, wiser and smarter than me, I should have done better. In afterthought, many of my painful lessons may have been avoided.

In the early 60's our house needed a new tar and gravel roof. Dad warned us to stay clear of the edges of the roof line in light of the fact hot tar was being applied. I chose not to heed the warning and ran right under the edge, the wind caught some of the hot tar, it landed on my brow, the side of my nose and my chin. At 8 years, old as well as the fright, it was painful and brought out a loud ouch. After the pain went away, the scars disappeared as well.

On an occasion a couple of years later, along with a friend I decided to build a rope swing in a live oak in the front yard. Dad saw me taking the rope and cautioned me against wrapping it around me in any manner. Climbing the tree, I wrapped the rope around a limb and then around my chest, I promptly slipped off the limb, the rope broke my fall as it caught and tightened around my neck. My friend was very quick to get under me, so I could loosen the rope and keep from hanging.

We had stairs in the house and had repeated instructions not to run up or down them. There was a time my sister aggravated me to the point of me chasing her, about the second step down, I tripped and got to the bottom very quickly only to be stopped by the corner of the wall. This brought my first emergency room visit, 3 stiches, several days' headache and a commitment to self to never run on the stairs again.

As I look back on my life, there is so much that qualifies as influences that contribute to who I have become. Regretfully some lessons had to be painful as I guess we can all be "know it all" at times. With so many positive influences many can think that a person gifted with so much good growing up, would surely live a model life. As I finish this chapter, it is with the question maybe many of us ask ourselves.

How often in retrospect do we see more clearly some lessons that could have been much less painful if we had just listened to the advice of others? My thoughts are that maybe the whole course of my life would have changed.

This chapter is dedicated to my friend little Johnny. After the estrangement of our relationship for many years, we became very close again. I admired the character of the man in his battle against cancer. He lost that battle yet gained eternity with His Savior – Jesus.

CHAPTER 3
EDUCATION RELIGION BOUNDARIES

I n an effort to connect the dots of the different periods of time that have had a distinct influence on my life, I need to speak of these periods. These are times of education, religious influence and the boundaries whether just implied or real that accompanied those seasons.

Growing up in Southport, a small southern town, sheltered us from some of the life lessons of the era. Our lessons went much further than just your basic reading, writing and arithmetic. My thoughts are, for me basic learning began at about five plus years old with life experiences.

Southport High School was the center of life in our small town. So many of our activities were based around the school. Sports, drama, Glee Club, and Sock Hops all added to the experience of growing up. All of our teachers were known around the town, some enjoyed a rather colorful persona and fed into some great gossip. Never- the- less, we didn't realize how much the simple nature of Southport and the time would be looked back on and cherished. The world many of us experienced growing up is a place we wish we could experience again.

GRADE SCHOOL

As a first grader in 1960, my early life heartthrob and I were named the class mascots. I still don't know what that meant. In my younger years, I was called Tommy to avoid confusion in the home as Dad and I had the same name. Not sure he wanted there to be any credit given him for some of my early year's mischief.

The first through sixth grades flew by. Our school days started with the Pledge of Allegiance and the Lord's Prayer. Prayer in school was very important to me. I was in constant prayer that Mom and Dad would not hear of my misbehaviors before I could come up with a good story. Also, areas of constant prayer were passing tests, doing homework and having all A's and B's on my report card. Many times, my prayers were answered. When they weren't, the "board of education" which is also known as a paddling board, was applied to my seat of learning.

My siblings and I loved our brown paper bag lunches. Many days I traded with others, so I could eat the goodies Mom didn't consider healthy. On special occasions, we had school lunches which were good. Southport High School had the best lunches ever, at least we thought so. They sure knew how to fry chicken, make meat loaf, spaghetti, collards, lima beans, cabbage, biscuits and cornbread. The consensus favorite was the chocolate oatmeal type cookies. As these ladies cooked and the aromas filled the school, it sure was hard to concentrate on our studies.

We were assigned seats in school. My seat was very seldom to my liking. I was usually right in the middle of the room. This was meant to keep my attention inside the room, not day dreaming looking out the windows. There was also an attempt to keep all the "class clowns" in the room separated. Needless to say, we still found ways to get into mischief. I still have a pencil lead in my upper left leg as a result of sword fighting with pencils.

Good behavior was rewarded with longer playground time. We had all the basics; swing sets, sliding boards, and a spinning platform. We played hop scotch, jump rope and the best game of the era, marbles. A good day of marbles was evidenced by overflowing pants packets. Those were some very good days.

As I grew older and looked forward to Junior High, the thought of being a teenager was exciting. The older I grew, so grew my capacity to learn new activities and the potential for unrealized fun. The first through sixth grades were good, I did learn our lessons of school and of life as well. My Aunt BecBec, was a great pianist, she served the church in that manner and also gave lessons. Since we were family, she offered piano lessons to my sibling's and myself as well. She learned quickly that nine-year-old boys, like myself, were better suited to play baseball and marbles. Having pockets full of marbles, made it very tough for me to sit through an hour long piano lesson.

One thing I did enjoy learning during this time in life was kissing. My close friend lived very close by and we would rendez-vous beside the water pump house in her side yard and spend hours practicing our new favorite pastime. I was not sure if I did it right, but it sure was fun practicing.

JUNIOR HIGH

At Southport High, we had an accelerated class. I'm still not sure how I ended up in there. The class was a combination of seventh and eighth grades. To fully understand this class, I need to share the story about a teacher. We'll call her Ms. Jones. She was older, single, and tough as nails. She liked keeping a bottle of alcohol in her top left-hand drawer. Many days around lunch time she would start taking sips from it. After making our assignments in the after-noon, she would get sleepy. It seemed she would sleep sitting up with her head on her hand. As we watched her intently, her head would do this bounce and then she would snore. We would com-plete many of our assignments on the black-board behind her. On one occasion with Ms. Jones sound asleep, "the class clown" was behind her at the black board and accidentally bumped the back of her head and to all our surprise, her hair turned around, completely covering her face. Not exactly sure what was going on another well-meaning young man in the class slammed a book on the floor. She woke up quickly and appeared lost, mumbled a few choice words, and fixed her hair. We never knew she wore a wig. Good thing was, with her vision impaired as it was, she was never able to identify the culprit. She was also not able to see us falling over in laughter. This image has always remained in my memory bank.

Ms. Jones also had a very strong arm. She could throw a black board eraser accurately and very fast. When we dozed off or mis-behaved in class, we experienced a big, white, chalky mark some-where on our body. She was also skilled at hitting moving targets. When my clothes bore those marks, my parents knew I needed some extra discipline. I would be back to pulling weeds and or sitting carefully for several days.

One day, when Ms. Jones escorted one of our misbehaving classmates to the principal's office, we checked her bottle for her. It didn't smell like water to us, we decided to do her a favor and poured it out. We replaced it with fresh water. Upon her return from the principal's office she opened her drawer, pulled out the drink bottle, and took a very big drink. I'm not sure how to describe her reaction, as I had never seen a look like that on a person's face before or since then. I think that was the first and maybe the only day she did not fall asleep in class.

HIGH SCHOOL

I started high school in 1968. Even though we were still in the same school, the doors to our future seemed to open a bit wider. The walks to and from school were pretty much the same. The invention of a new challenge awaited us many days as we crossed Bonnets' Creek. A large culvert ran under Moore Street for the creek to flow through. The challenge was to run from end- to- end and from side to side without getting wet- this was called "doobying." I'm not sure how to gauge the success of it as for some reason we would end up wet and muddy.

Officially being a High School student now allowed us to leave school grounds for lunch. There was only one cool place to go for lunch, Oliver's Grill. They had the absolute best burger of any type you could ever get your mouth around. There was no graceful way to devour one of these delicacies. The burgers were so juicy that you wore them from cheek- to- cheek and the juice ran down to your elbows. It was nothing fancy- just the best burger ever. The chocolate shakes and malts were the perfect complement to those burgers too. When Oliver's closed, so ended a great Southport tradition.

During the late sixties, no town was complete without a teen hangout. We had the Teen Scene. It was complete with a soda and nab bar, pool tables, a juke- box and a dance floor. Guys would dress in our favorite madras slacks, blue shirt and penny loafers- complete with dimes. Girls would wear skirts, sweaters, bobby socks and tennis shoes. The place rocked to the beats of the Beatles, Herman's Hermits, Junior Walker and the All Stars, The Tams, The Temptations, The Drifters, The Monkees and so many more. The music influenced our best moves: The Shag, The Watusi, The Twist, and the Cha-ha.

Schools in Southport integrated in 1968 as well. Three black students came to school with us and it was great. Many of us wondered why it hadn't happened sooner. We realized that we weren't different, especially in our hopes for a better world.

Our freshman year in high school was interrupted by a fire that destroyed the school that was built in 1922.

After the fire, we attended school many places in downtown Southport. One of these places was Southport Baptist Church, right beside City Park. The City Park was the home of the famous hand crank water pump. Stories have it, if you drink the water from the pump, you will always come back to Southport- seems to have worked for me. This park has always been full of azaleas, dogwoods, camellias and very large pretty live oaks. This made it easy to get lost on the way to class and end up twenty miles away at Long Beach Pier. I'm not sure, but for some reason many of us felt surfing was mandatory. Any rate, many of us excelled at it, but regretfully our report cards did not reflect these achievements.

School was not terrible. As many of us look back and would enjoy the chance to experience some of these days again. We had great teachers and no matter our thoughts of them at the time, they really did care for us. To this day, Mrs. Cheryl Shew is a very active encourager in my life. In my 9th grade she came to Southport fresh out of college. Not sure she was fully aware of all she was in for upon arrival. She was young, beautiful, single and most importantly, a fine Christian lady. We put her through a lot in every means possible to rattle her. We probably did upset her at times. Her love of God was her strength and through it all, she stayed and continued to be a very positive influence on so many students. Today she remains in Southport and is a wonderful witness of the love of God to many. God bless you Mrs. Shew and speaking for many, thanks so much for having faith in us and being so supportive to us in life. We love you so much.

The end of the summer of sixty-nine brought many changes, some quite dramatic. With the burning of Southport High, I started my sophomore year in a fully integrated school. The school that had been the black school in town is where we all went. Things started out good. We had the first high school football team in several years. This team provided a uniting influence on us. I played on the team and quickly found football to be my favorite team sport. We weren't the best team, but we did have fun. When the photographer showed up to take pictures, he announced all the previous had been color pictures, now he was taking the back and white. We all chuckled when a black team mate asked, "What's the difference, they are all going to be black and white anyway?"

Shortly thereafter, insults and racist remarks started, and physical fights began. It was sad to see the deep wounds that many years of racism produced. With all the trouble at school there were several of us that ended up at Long Beach Pier and spent our days surfing, the perfect place of peace and solitude in a very troubled community. I got credit for attending fifty-two days of school that year. By some miraculous occurrence, I ended up on the National Honor Society and passed the tenth grade. Looking back at that year, we had some good relationships that started growing with friends of the opposite race and still did not understand how all this strife had to carry on. Seems that there were just those that thrived on unrest – those of both races. To say that these were turbulent days is an accurate assessment.

My parents were not impressed with my lack of attendance in public school. My parents, with other concerned parents, got together and made the decision to send me with eleven other truants to Frederick Military Academy in Portsmouth, Virginia. This was six hours away from home. I'm not sure any of us were ready for the wake-up call that awaited us.

The end of the summer 1970 was upon us and the start of my junior year was in no way what I considered as ideal. I arrived at Frederick a couple of weeks early to play football. This brought a crash course in expected Military behavior. Saluting guys younger than me from the start did not sit well with me. We had three football practices daily with the first being at 5:30am. I learned very quickly the proper way to respond to a bugle blowing reveille. At that point, I questioned if that was what I really signed up for. After football practice, we were taught how to spit shine our shoes, polish our brass, tie our ties, and how to properly wear our uniforms. Then came the fun part, how to properly clean our rooms for a full white glove inspection. Did I fail to mention personal appearance – complete with shaved head?

During football, I suffered a dislocated right shoulder. It limited my ability to salute the younger, smaller officers. Many of them didn't appreciate that I didn't salute them. When my shoulder healed, and the sling was gone, at times, I failed to remember the expected protocol and didn't salute. Demerits were the penalty which led to penalty tours. A penalty tour was one hour marching a forty-yard path, back and forth, with a M-16 on my healing shoulder. After about twenty hours marching, my memory of proper protocol was restored.

I lived in a room with three other first year cadets. At times, we had weekend leave. We never failed to make the most of those weekends. During those weekends, I first learned to like drinking beer and in retrospect regretfully, was introduced to marijuana.

I'm not exactly sure how they determined who would be roommates, but chemistry in our room was interesting – literally. One of my roommates was good in chemistry and loved mixing chemicals. On one occasion, he snuck some stuff out of the lab with the intention of making flares. He brought them back to our room and started mixing. One roommate was very interested and watched. The other roommate was on front gate guard duty. I was following the rules for our enforced study hall and doing my homework. I was blissfully unaware of what was taking place behind me. It seems the mixing was taking place in our empty brasso can. To ensure the brightest possible flare, he wanted the chemicals packed in as full as possible. To achieve that level of fullness, he banged the can against his desk surface. Unbeknownst to the chemist, the concoction became combustible with friction, which led to an explosion. The bottom of the can blew off, nearly castrating him. The watching roommate caught the exploding chemicals from his chin to his waist as the can split open. As an eight-foot fireball flowed through the room, my back and shoulders received second and third-degree burns. Our absentee roommate that was on guard duty was quite surprised as fire trucks showed up asking directions to Welton Hall room 4A. We all survived the experience. The one most seriously burned was in the hospital about two weeks. The chemist, very thankful to still have his family jewels, was hospitalized overnight. My burns were treated at our infirmity and healed nicely. Last, I heard, the one on guard duty had several rounds of shock therapy and is doing well. The chemist and other burn victim were dismissed from the school a short time after the incident. Our halls all had mottos for each year: interestingly for Welton Hall, ours was, "Chemistry can be exciting!"

The platoon I was in was Henry Church Rifles. We were the precision drill team. We marched in parades and put on exhibitions showcasing our skills with handling an M-16 rifle. We spent a lot of time in practice as we spun, tossed with spins and exchanged arms with spins. It was fun and provided a great sense of achievement when we got it right injury free.

Bible classes were a part of our education. It was a very strong plus for my parents when they made their decision for me to attend. We had a very godly man, Major Wilbur Presson, as our instructor. Given the environment and the time in history, his task was monumental. We had chapel on Sunday mornings as well. He was then, and still is in my opinion, one of the best teachers and preachers I have ever known.

As the name of the school implies, we had military training as well. Military science was part of our classroom curriculum. We experienced what the war in Vietnam looked like in films and pictures- some of those sights were gruesome. We were taught how to formulate actual battle plans under varying conditions and different enemy approaches. There were several cadets with a weaker tolerance and did not fare well in those classes. We had weapons and arms training. I achieved pro-marksman in firing a rifle accurately. In hind sight that was pretty tough training for fourteen to twenty-year old's.

On the sadder side of this was the fact, guys that had just graduated were going to Vietnam fighting and dying. Lt. Col. Alvis T. Barrington, Battalion Commander at Frederick Military Academy 1969-1970 was killed in action Vietnam 1971. He was the top ranked cadet and many of us knew him. When the announcement was made to us, we all felt sadness and grief. Many of us also wondered what he died for.

My senior year came with many more privileges at school. We were living in a season of a lot of change. The preparation for the future, and college was upon us. Gardner – Webb College fit the criteria my parents desired for me. It just so happened the school was interested in my football skills as well. While travelling to the college with my Mom and Dad, they became very concerned about me when we discussed marijuana, my view was not in line with theirs.

During my Senior year, I played football and became a platoon leader of Henry Church Rifles. We were able to have weekends to enjoy the Tidewater area of Virginia. There were parades and events we as Cadet Corps participated in. As we marched in parades with streets lined with people, our character could be tested. There were anti-war protestors that saw us as military. At times, they would physically challenge our presence. It was a violation for those folks to attempt to break our ranks. To prevent people from charging us, breaking our ranks, and to protect our cadets the order to spin arms was given. While marching the rifles would then be spun. To the dismay of some protestors they felt the impact of a spinning M-16 crashing into them as they attempted to break our ranks.

Yes, 1972 was a year of change for all of us. The formal dances, drama presentations, sports achievements, academic pursuits and college campus visits kept our plates full. I spent a lot of time in study. My behavior was much better in my senior year. I earned Honor Cadet status all year long. This status was awarded to Cadets with no demerits and an A average in academics. My parents and I were proud.

The classes all had their own special flavor. Major Tex Lindsay was an expert in History and quite the character. I can still hear him say," Sit up in your seat son, you look like a wet dish rag."

Major Gelback taught civics and government, and was very patriotic. We had a cadet Harvey, fondly remembered as the class antagonist. He knew just how to question Major Gelback to get the maximum response. We all learned from Harvey not to question Maj. Gelback in any type of humorous way about any of our founding fathers.

Captain Bert Morrison was our very colorful senior English teacher. Not sure if he ever really understood me. He signed my 1972 yearbook, "Thank-you for helping me appreciate the true merits of a Southport existence." I'm still not sure what he was saying, but you know, Southport is a great place.

Captain Rose was my French teacher. I did very well in my written work, I always got an A. He just seemed to never understand me when I spoke French. It was most likely the result of my heavy southern accent.

Finally, was Lieutenant Gibbs, my football coach and physical education teacher. He believed the cure for any short comings or losses was to run, we ran a lot.

Our school President Colonel Philip G Inscoe was made of the finest qualities and always had a kind and encouraging word for us each.

Lieutenant Colonel Robert C. Plaine was our commandant. I got to spend time with him when demerits and penalty tours were issued. He was a tough disciplinarian. Under his steady influence, many boys became men of character and integrity.

We did have fun at Frederick. We had a cadet captain who owned a MGB that was properly parked in the cadet parking lot nightly. For some odd reason about five of us thought it would look good parked in the middle of our parade ground. Shortly after taps, we all snuck out, picked it up, and carried it to the parade ground and left it. The next morning at reveille the cadet captain was greeted with the sight of his car in the middle of the area through which we marched to breakfast. Our friend had some explaining to do, seems as if he did it well. We never heard of anyone marching penalty tours for it.

We had a barber, Mr. Mac McKinney and he was very skilled at keeping our hair cut properly – military standard. There was a supply hall that handled all our personal needs, laundry, light bulbs, brasso, floor wax, shoe polish and toilet paper. When it was time for more toilet paper, the saying was "no hub, no rub." We had to turn in the empty hub to get a new roll as it was discovered the old hub could be modified to be a pipe to smoke pot in.

Many lasting relationships were formed at Frederick as well as life lessons. A lifelong friend of mine from Southport, Steve Gainey, attended Frederick as well. Steve had an aunt in Norfolk, Aunt Wilma. Aunt Wilma would open her home to many of us on the weekends. She was the mother away from home that I needed. She would provide an ear to listen and a shoulder to cry on often. Yep, I got homesick and missed my mom often. Aunt Wilma was a great cook and always fed us well. Her amazing meals were just what we needed, appreciated, and looked forward to. I have had opportunity to see her at times over the years, she is still a lovely lady with a great Christian spirit that I will always love and respect.

My years at Frederick did include my introduction to marijuana. What started out so innocently with friends just having fun opened the door to many more very serious consequences later on in my life.

Graduation in May 1972 was a great experience. There were new doors to freedom and more independence from home. The independence from family was rapidly approaching.

In August 1972, I made the trip across the state of North Carolina to the foothills and a small Baptist College, Gardner – Webb. The intention, with a partial scholarship, was to play football and pursue an education aimed at preparing me for the full-time ministry. Spiritually, I was in no place to be a minister of the Gospel message of Jesus Christ. Gardner - Webb had many rules. At that point in my life, with a new-found freedom, no reveille to wake me up or taps to signal lights out, no set uniform, I would come and go as I pleased. It did not take long to start making some bad choices.

I took all the standard freshman courses. Those classes did include some ministry training. My life was in no way a good witness and it did bother me to be living such a hypocritical life.

The girls at Gardner-Webb had a curfew – the guys didn't. When the girls went in, the guys often got up to no good. One of our favorite activities was popular in that era was panty raids. After the girls being settled in for a couple of hours, some of us hound dogs would park under their windows. We would shout for them to throw down their panties, not sure if we achieved greater manhood or not, it was something to do. The window I chose, the girl co-operated. My first trophy was a pair of panties with Monday monogrammed on them - it worked the first time, many times later upon return to the same window, I was equally successful. I ended up with panties for every day of the week. Sadly, I never met the girl who owned them either, maybe that was a good thing.

Boones Farm Wine was a cheap and trendy drink at the time. Under the influence of that and pot, there were several of us who chose to expand on our variety of extra-curricular activities. Instead of risking getting caught smoking pot and drinking on campus we would take a ride out into the nearby country. There were plenty of dirt roads and fields full of cattle. While out one day on a narrow dirt road with a bridge over a creek we saw a man, who looked fresh out of the movie "Deliverance" fishing in the creek. We stopped and watched. We were stoned, so it did not take much to get and hold our attention. As we watched, he pulled out a pouch of tobacco to roll a cigarette. The process included placing the rolling paper, gummed edge down and creasing it between his fourth finger and little finger. He then filled the crease with tobacco. He quickly gave it a bit of a roll between his fingers, licked the gummed edge, very quickly with his opposite hand in a downward motion and on one movement produced a perfectly rolled cigarette ready to smoke. In our stoned state, we were amazed. We saw the merit in his skill and asked if he would teach us. He agreed. After looking at our tobacco and declaring how he had never seen that type tobacco before the teaching process began. After several smacks of the hand, a valiant effort in which we lost half our stash, we thanked him and moved on.

While driving the country roads, we often pulled over to admire the scenery. On one such occasion a small herd of beef cattle came to check us out. There were four of us and we all became a bit annoyed by their stares. Over the fence we went, and the chase was on. Given it was afternoon, the fear of being caught set in. We all decided that doing this in the dark was the safer, better option. Very seldom were there good outcomes to decisions made by four stoners. After a couple of weeks of no success in chasing the cows in the dark, falling in ditches, tripping over rocks, running into fences we never saw and of course running through you know what. We found a loading pen full of cows. This was ideal, at least we thought so. We could herd them into a much smaller loading pen, get a couple to walk up to the loading ramp. We would then place our legs on each side of the ramp and have a guy get in front of cow and walk them back. We would sit down on the cow, they instantly objected to our being on their backs and we were thrown. We would land with laughs and shouts.

That area of North Carolina has very orange clay mud. The melting winter snow combined with the mud produced a slippery mess. Slipping, sliding and falling in this had a very detrimental impact on our clothes. When not trying to ride the animals, we took our shots at tackling them. We spent much time in the mixture as they stepped on us, kicked us, head butted us and yes, other things on us as well. Coming home for a weekend visit, I presented Mom with my laundry. Not sure I will ever forget the look on Mom's face as she gazed upon the pile of what used to be nice, new school clothes. She was not happy. I gave the best explanation possible, not sure that helped. I explained to her that I had joined a fraternity. I felt a thigh, which included riding, tackling and pulling a tail hair from a cow. That made things worse. My parents mutually agreed they did not send me to college to learn to ride cows. From then on, I used old clothes and the school laundromat.

Gardner-Webb was a great place to go to school, if only I had focused on what I was there for. I did participate in some weekend ministry trips and did preach a few Sunday sermons. As I look back I experienced great guilt as I understood the level of hypocrisy in my life. After meeting with a staff ministerial leader, it became

30

clear to me, many of the other areas in my life were not secret. I had a scripture spoken to me that was very timely and accurate. Numbers 32:23, "But if you fail to do this, you will be sinning against the Lord, and you may be sure that your sin will find you out." I could not have it both ways. My grade point average suffered, and I suffered. The beginning of a rapid downward spiral was upon me. I was running from God when I left Gardner-Webb in May of 1973.

Upon arriving home for the summer of 1973 was when my Christian upbringing no longer influenced me. The mandatory church attendance of my youth, Frederick Military Academy, and Gardner-Webb were options I rebelled against.

The boundaries that living a Christian life represented to me were totally compromised. The sudden state of being nineteen years old, and smarter than everyone else (so I thought) led to a desire for greater independence than what I had already experienced. I was becoming fiercely rebellious. I had a job, a car, and a house with friends offered to me. I could choose, and I did. I made the worst possible choice I could. I rejected God, family, education, and boundaries in order to live in full rebellion to everything that had been instilled in my life since birth. Interesting in writing this chapter how often the word I is used. Yep it was-all about me.

CHAPTER 4
REBELLION, HAVING FUN AND FEELING GOOD

L ooking back at many years' worth of memories, I am increasingly more aware of how my journey took the path it did. There
were many different people and places that had an impact on me.
There were many positive influences by so many growing up in an
iconic small-town environment. Where did all the unraveling start
that became such a mess.

From an early age, it seems we all have this inherent ability
to make choices that fly fully in the face of how we are advised.
Seems as time passed I was increasingly more able to become a
rule unto myself. John Calvin, once said; "For there is no one so
great or mighty that he can avoid the misery that will rise up against
him when he resists and strives against God'" The more I grew,
the more I became convinced I was smarter than those leading and
teaching me. It dawns on me now, I was living in rebellion against
pretty much everyone and everything that represented authority in
my life, God included.

Psalms 107:17-18; "Some were fools through their sinful ways
and because of their iniquities suffered affliction; they loathed any
kind of food and they drew near to the gates of death" This passage
pretty much sums up these years in my life.

Growing up in the sixties and seventies it seems the influence
of the culture was to rebel. Much of the rebellion had no just cause,
it seems as if it was just what we were supposed to do. The results
of many of our rebellious behaviors, in the end made us appear
quite foolish.

Trying to address when my rebellious nature began, I look to my childhood years. Our parents encouraged us not to play with matches. I could not wait for a chance to play with matches. The opportunity soon presented itself. Being the small-town Southport was, Mom did her major grocery shopping in Wilmington about forty-five minutes away. We had a black lady, Alneta that helped around the house and looked after us when Mom was out at times. One of these days as Mom was away and Alneta was looking after us presented the perfect opportunity to play with matches. My younger sibling and I were in our parents' bedroom, that was a no-no. Mom and Dad had a wicker trash can and it was full of paper. We decided this was an opportune time to experiment with matches. We took the trash can out in the back yard – at just the perfect eye level to view out of the kitchen window. Alneta just happened to have a view out of the window as she was ironing. We both lit matches that landed by some strange happening in the trash can. The resulting fire was quite impressive, we had not figured on the wicker basket burning as well. Thankfully a very startled Alneta responded very quickly with a nearby hose and the fire was extinguished. Mom would bring us Cracker-Jacks for our good behaviors while she was gone shopping. After Alneta shared our exploits with Mom we did not get any Cracker-Jacks that day, in fact Mom gave them to Alneta to take to her children. We were not happy with this action of Mom and we were even less pleased when Dad got home. We sat very gingerly for a few days afterwards.

Being disobedient did have consequences. As we each look back on our lives, can we see where acts of disobedience actually fed into a growing spirit of rebellion? As a child, there were so many times when I felt the urge to do things and was just not wise enough to consider the teaching to not do such things. In learning to ride a bicycle we were taught what the handle bars were for. The challenge to ride without using the handle bars was greater than the desire to obey. After many falls, bloody elbows, hands and knees it became obvious, it was much less painful to use the handle bars.

I was brought up in an alcohol-free home, neither of my parents drank. At fifteen years old it was time for me to experiment with beer. Pabst Blue Ribbon and Schlitz were popular beers of the era, it was time to try. I did not like that taste of beer, may have been an early sign to stay away. My remedy was then to drink fast. The result was, I got to feeling very good very quickly, followed very quickly by being very sick.

Upon turning eighteen so much of life changed, I could drink legally, vote, and sign up for the draft. I was not in favor of the Vietnam War. Too many friends had died or been wounded for life there; many of us never really understood why. The manifestation of my rebellion to the war was to register as a conscientious objector. This was a process where in several interviews I had the opportunity to express my views, in the end I was classified as CO as my draft status. On record, I made it clear, If America is attacked, I will be first in line to defend our country, I feel the same way today.

After going to college and coming home in the summer of 1973 rebellion really took over. Southport was the location Carolina Power and Light Company chose to build a nuclear power plant. There were many job opportunities paying very good money. I applied for and got what was meant to be a summer job. My day started early by getting up to go to work. After work a quick stop at the house to change into my surfing shorts, grab my board and off to the beach. After a couple of joints and surfing till dark, I would head home. Mom and Dad did not approve of this schedule for me and voiced it. My response was very quick and not thought out at all. I moved out. There was a four-bedroom house at the beach, three of my friends lived in and needed another to help pay the rent. I was officially independent – no rules- just rights.

As construction for the power plant continued many of the employees came from Texas and Mexico. Many of these employees had drug connections which flowed into our area. The opportunity to sell drugs was there for me and I took it. The money from the job and selling drugs, plus independence and loving the lifestyle led to some very bad decisions, the worst decision I ever made was to reject my parents and their wishes for me by choosing not to go back to Gardner-Webb College the fall of 1974.

Staying stoned, partying and surfing was not exactly role model example for a big brother. My parents were concerned for all their children equally. I fully understood them not wanting me to be a bad influence on my brothers. I do regret losing so many years with them growing up.

One of the characteristics of my rebellion was anyone who spoke to me in any manner about my out of control life style, immediately became my enemy. My parents were still concerned for me and spoke to me about my life, this just further estranged me from them as well.

I was partying every day, making money and having a whole lot of fun- so I thought. The most applicable definition of rebellion that fits where I was, is: the action or process of resisting authority, control or convention. Synonyms are: defiance, disobedience, insubordination, subversion, resistance.

As we look more closely at how all this can happen in one person's life, it helps to look at it from the spiritual point of view. To make an honest assessment of where we are in life, we first must be open to accept correction and not rebel or be defensive towards those who love you the most. The spirit of rebellion is so subtle in how it gains a foot hold in our lives. Anything that we allow in our lives will grow to a point to where if unchecked or not dealt with will lead us to greater levels of compromise, rebellion, rationalization, justification and the list goes on. If you do not stand for something you will fall for anything.

In the early stages of my life, the disobedience to my parents seemed minor at the time. My continuing to live in that manner of rejection of Godly wisdom and authority caught up with me. Whether the hot tar off the roof, falling down the stairs or wrecking on my bike, they all hurt. My desire to drink, smoke pot did in fact lead me to harder drugs. I was not doing this to escape personal pain, I was doing it solely to have fun and feel good. What was culturally acceptable behavior and morals very quickly were compromised with the, if it feels good, "do it" mentality. To the younger readers of this book, let me encourage you, be careful of things you see as little, giving in to them, over the years leads to bigger mistakes with more dire consequences.

The mind set of party, party, party on New Year's Eve, Fourth of July, Birthdays, celebrations of any sorts can get out of control, party mentality can and does on occasion have tragic outcomes. Even as I write this chapter a friend lost her early thirty's daughter. The daughter a young, attractive, professional went out for a night of drinks a few lines of cocaine and fun. Upon arriving home took a Xanax, was dead a couple of hours later. Sadly, when talking with her mom, the mother had no idea the daughter used cocaine. None of us are bullet proof no matter the false sense of strength a high gives us.

For me it is very challenging to remember many of the past memorable occasions in my life. Having so much fun and feeling so good often led to me saying things and or doing things that hurt others. Seeing some of these people later in life has had varying results and responses. Be careful when you are having fun and feeling good, you may say or do something to another who does not see it the same way and harbor hurt towards you for many years.

In a state of rebellion my favorite friend was denial. There was no one that could convince me that what I saw as feeling good and having fun was wrong. Moving from smoking pot to taking hallucinogenic drugs produced a major difference in the effect on the mind and body. The effect of the hallucinogens was in reality the body's reaction to ingesting poison. Long term physical damage is done to the body and mind. There were a couple of trips on LSD that were bad, if anyone ever experiences a bad trip, the description is no way fun. These trip type drugs usually had some type of amphetamine added to keep you up longer and give the drug a bit more kick. There may have been a feeling of euphoria for several hours, that was followed by several hours of being wired and then the crash, most often that is exactly what if felt like as well; A CRASH!!

This chapter may not seem exactly like what you expected, don't feel surprised it isn't what I expected either. This state of mind, the rebellion, having fun and feeling good represented a dramatic change from the innocence of where my life began. After a certain point, each and every day was filled with many illegal activities.

The behavior had now become more compulsive than being rationally thought out. The fun and feeling good had moved from being wisely planned to what best worked for the moment. There was not reasoning or rationale to life. The simplistic approach to having fun was now borderline insanity. Very quickly life can go from fun to dangerous if we fail to address the simplest manifestation of rebellion in our lives.

My personal rebellion was hidden, it was overshadowed by having fun and feeling good. The same areas of life I placed so much emphasis on for my personal expression of freedom were now the same things that challenged my very freedom.

My family and friends no longer knew me and even worse, could not trust me. What became even worse, I did not have a clue any longer as to who I was. Places where I had felt safe were no longer safe. People I dealt drugs with were getting in trouble and to lessen their own troubles would give information which led to others being arrested. This ended up being deadly to some and meant hard time in prison to others.

Yep, rebellion, having fun and feeling good was beginning to be a very real fight for life. Life- death- jails- institutions are the outcomes for many of us that live-in rebellion that results in denial. Denial is one of the first identifiable behaviors of an addictive life style. What could possibly come next?

CHAPTER 5
BLUE LIGHTS, BADGES AND JAIL

One thing for certain about life, our actions based on decisions have consequences, some may be good, some may be bad, others are just totally caution to the wind. They can lead to a lifestyle, a very risky lifestyle.

In the summer of 1973 when my awareness of my independence kicked in, so did my ability to start making terrible decisions. As my life went from one party to the next, my use of drugs and alcohol increased. It did not take long to realize that lifestyle was not cheap.

A strong misconception with those who locally sold drugs was that if they involved me, I would not get in trouble since my dad was the mayor of Southport. That couldn't have been more wrong! My dad always told me that if I got into trouble he would not get me out of it, and for a year there was no trouble.

In the summer of 1974, I became aware of the police having knowledge of my illegal activities. One evening at home, I was partying with two friends and the wall of the house lit up with flashing blue lights. At first, we were thinking these lights were hallucinations brought on by the LSD we did. These lights had a loud knock on the door. We did not recognize that sound as being a part of the song Quadrophonic by Foghat that we were grooving out to.

Reality that it was the police at my door set in quickly. The realization was followed by acute paranoia. I ran to the bathroom and flushed drugs immediately. Then, in an altered state of awareness, I answered the door. There were at least ten police officers with guns drawn, demanding to know my evening's activities. I am sure my demeanor made them aware of my mental state. Apparently, they had gone to make a drug bust which turned in to an exchange of gunfire and the culprits getting away. After they checked the hoods of our cars and finding the engines cool, they determined it wasn't me and they left without searching my home. That night, I realized they were aware of my activities and where I lived. My life immediately changed, and I knew I had to be more careful.

Later in 1974, there was a shortage of marijuana. An older man, with a questionable reputation, approached me with an offer to give me enough marijuana to sell for a couple of weeks. I had to make a two-hour trip to pick up the marijuana. We went in a different car to avoid any suspicion. A friend, aware of the car I went in, stopped us before we made it back to the house. The friend informed me that my house was staked out, so we immediately stashed the dope.

Not long after I got home, the police showed up with a search warrant for the exact amount I had picked up. I realized the man who set up the drop was working with the police. I did have dope in the house, and the police found it. I was arrested on November 15, 1974. I was charged with felony possession with the intent to sell marijuana. I very quickly made bond. Even after being arrested, I didn't learn a lesson.

A few weeks later, I sold some speed to a couple of folks who had been breaking and entering cottages on the beach. The detectives caught them, but they were offered a deal in exchange for information. They gave the police my name and told them I had been selling speed. A little over a month since my first arrest, the police showed up at my house once again with a search warrant and found my stash of speed. On December 27, 1974, I was arrested and charged with felony possession of amphetamines with the intent to sell. My bond was set much higher the second time and I couldn't make bail. Several people thought about bailing me out, but my dad visited these folks and asked them not to post my bail. He hoped I would learn a lesson if I had to stay in jail.

I spent twenty-five days in a small jail cell, which only held four people. One guy had been arrested for murdering his wife. He chain smoked non-filtered cigarettes and drank a jar of instant coffee a day. Needless to say, he was very high strung. In conversation one day he casually informed me, "If you wake up in the middle of the

night with my hands around your throat, don't take it personally."
He further explained to me that he had internal demons that he had
not yet come to terms with. That led me to question the sanity of
the choices and how I had ended up next to that man in a jail cell.
He was soon relocated to a state mental prison after I discussed the
conversation with the jailer.

On my twenty sixth day in jail, I went to court to face my
charges. Upon the advice of my father and attorney, I plead guilty
and the asked for the mercy of the court. The district attorney and
judge were both men my father knew well, I got a very severe
scolding from each. The judge then announced my sentence. His
words, "I am sentencing you to three years," turned my mind into
a calculator. Based on jail house knowledge, three years meant
about one and a half years in prison. Then the judge spoke again,
"Three years on each charge." That meant three years in prison. I
wouldn't get out until I was twenty- five years old. After another
pause, the judge spoke again, "Considering you have no previous
record, I am suspending those sentences and giving you a three
years' probation."

I exited the courthouse a free man for the first time in twenty-six
days feeling the weight off my shoulders. The probation officer
set out my rules and expected behavior and I was back to life with
some regulation. As one of the requirements, I had to get a job. So,
I got a job in a favorite Italian restaurant in town.

We had a varied clientele, which included police officers. One
evening two officers came and ordered a large pepperoni pizza.
I'm not sure what came over me, but while making their pizza I
placed a slice of jalapeno pepper, under each piece of pepperoni. I
watched the officers, whom I knew, eat their pizza. I noticed their
tea glasses emptying rather quickly. Their faces grew redder and
sweat poured from their brows. Once they realized what was going
on, they informed the owner of the restaurant. I guess the remaining
half of the pizza was given to me as severance pay.

Things got pretty hot for me at the beach and it was time for
me to move somewhere that my reputation wasn't as well known.
Moving while on probation takes permission from both the probation officer in the current location and the probation officer in the

new location. I got both of them to approve. The officer where I moved to had very little tolerance for drug dealers, especially from the beach. Upon settling in to my new digs, my old habits started again, which included dealing.

One night of laid-back partying, the partying was interrupted by a sharp knock on the door. My probation officer was standing at the door with a host of sheriff's deputies. They entered with search warrant in hand and as the house was dimly lit, they headed straight to a lamp which had a plastic container full of pot under it. By some strange occurrence, they laid the warrant on top and never saw the pot.

I also had some opium, which is very gummy- like tar. Without thinking, I rested my elbow right on top of it and it stuck to my shirt. While I was spared them finding the pot and the opium, my next concern was the two pounds of pot stashed in the middle of the brick steps they continued to walk over as the officers entered and left the house. I also had two gallons of marijuana tea in my refrigerator. After a couple of hours of searching, one of the dozen or so officers opened my refrigerator. Totally unaware, he asked for a glass of tea and without thinking, I said "yes." He remarked how good it was- a bit different- but good. The next thing I knew, all the officers had some tea. They had drunk all the evidence. When the search ended, and all the officers left, the search warrant still covered the container of pot, the two pounds of pot were still in the middle of the steps that the officers had walked over for three hours. The opium was stuck to the elbow of my shirt. That night was one of the only times the police came and went and didn't file charges against me.

From that point in time, I either got better at avoiding trouble or God spared me. I went six years without a single run-in with the police.

On January 27, 1982 I was at a party in Charleston, South Carolina and cocaine was the drug of choice for the evening. It was a large party and there were people I did not know. During the course of the evening, one of the party goers and myself started to talk. He told me that he dealt Quaaludes. As we talked, I asked to buy some from him and he obliged. Later that night, he asked if I would sell him some cocaine, so I did.

Several hours later, while leaving the party, I was approached by two plain clothes detectives and charged for selling to an officer. The man who sold me Quaaludes was a NARC. After a lengthy trial and a lot of money, I was found not guilty on a technicality.

During the next eight years, I was very careful about who I sold drugs to. I started to sell more cocaine than pot because there was more money in cocaine and it was less bulky. My personal drug of choice quickly became free base cocaine. My old habit quickly became a full addiction. I did not look or live like an addict. I dressed well, had a job and associated with people that could afford a couple of hundred dollars a day to party. These same people knew about my frequent trips to Florida, Jamaica, and the Bahamas. These people knew about the quality of my product and were always ready to pay. Life was good. I had a cover business working the beach services, and had a good circle of clients. I had no worries.

In all honesty, from the end of 1982 until the end of the summer 1986, my biggest decisions were whether I was going to a club or going to a house party. Close to the end of the summer of 1986, I made a bad decision to file a false police report concerning a missing Hobie cat. This caused an arrest  but was cleared up with replacing the boat. I realized the trouble my cocaine addiction was causing and quit using.

I moved back home to Southport from Charleston. I continued to deal cocaine and since drinking had never been an issue for me, I drank more. Then at thirty-two years old, I started my own restaurant. My style of cooking, which I learned in Charleston, Houma, and New Orleans, was quite popular. The business quickly expanded from one restaurant to four. Money was never an issue as my restaurants and drug money kept me happy.

I realized the police and a couple of other agencies knew I was up to something. It became clear that it was time to get out of the drug business. My decision to get out of the drug business was good, however, law enforcement had eyes on everything I did. The tax men came after me and did not let up.

My drinking increased and led to drinking and driving, which led to consequences. In 1990, I was arrested. That arrest snowballed several subsequent events in my life. Those events led me to pack up and run in an attempt to avoid prosecution. Alaska was my intended destination. I stopped in the North Carolina mountains to camp and fish a couple of days. I continued to drink a lot and made the mistake of being drunk in a public place. The police showed up to speak with me and I gave them an alias. At that time, I wasn't fully aware of the consequences I would experience from missing court appearances.

The next day the police showed again. They had established my identity and arrested me on a fugitive warrant. Police officers from Wilmington, North Carolina drove six hours to Boone, North Carolina and took me into custody. They drove me back in handcuffs to Wilmington where I remained in jail for a month before my trial.

I was found guilty of several money and tax charges. I served six months in prison and then my sentence was changed to probation. I was sentenced to five years of probation. At that point I had lost four restaurants, a couple of million dollars, two cars and basically everything I owned. I went from being a successful local restauranteur to broke, in jail, owing back taxes, social security, and several other people.

During probation, I had to work. I was supervised closely, and most of what I earned was garnished to pay my debts to society. The pressure on me, or should I say that I put on myself, led me to make more bad decisions. Along with drinking, I started smoking crack cocaine. I didn't consider myself an addict, but I spent money I didn't have and got back into dealing.

As I sit here and write this, I shake my head. Was I totally insane? I was paying my bills and living, but that was all it was. That season led me to depths of darkness I had never gone to.

I got a major break from some real estate investors that wanted me to manage their holdings for them. This included a home, a couple of work vehicles, and some dignity. It also took me away from dealing and crack cocaine. For a brief one-year period, I did very well. It seems prosperity was to be a short-lived experience. I again had drinking issues that led to bad choices. Those choices led to assault on a police officer, which led to other charges and continued probation. I faced a felony. The magistrate did not set a bond; I was in jail and held for a couple of months before my trial.

The judges and district attorneys were tired of seeing me. Since my past was well known and I was thirty-seven, my second chances ran out. My incarceration was a result of twenty-two years' worth of sentences with a three-year felony charge led to the pounding of the hammer of justice. On June 17, 1992, my years' worth of sentences, plus a new sentence for three years of felony charges were activated and I was sent to the maximum-security prison unit in Hoke County, North Carolina.

I was in jail for three months and now not sure at all as to how much of this sentence I would serve. After a full day of riding all over the state of North Carolina on a prison bus, dropping inmates at different prisons, we arrived at the Hoke County prison that would be my home for the next six weeks. As we entered the prison through three sets of locked gates, rows of fencing topped with razor wire, the high level security at the prison became apparent.

Twelve of us that were brought to the prison that day to be processed, and orient us to prison life. Upon entering, we were stripped, searched, and sprayed with hoses with a disinfectant shampoo to kill anything that may be on our bodies. After being issued prison clothes, we were marched down a long corridor full of inmates who eyed us up as we were led to the initial processing area. We were weighed, measured, finger printed and given physicals. All this took place in glass offices under the supervision of armed guards and inmates that had various interests in the new prisoners. After several hours of processing we were taken to a dining room, totally segregated from the rest of the prison population and fed our dinner.

My guess is all new prisoners were eyed very closely by the other inmates for many reasons. The prison had a ward for the criminally insane, which included people serving life sentences without possibility of parole. The prison housed pedophiles, murderers, rapists, and thieves.

Our dinner was a very bland cheese sandwich with a slice of processed meat and potato chips. After dinner, we were removed from the dining room surrounded by prison guards. We were informed this was for our protection because fresh meat was not safe unattended. It seemed like the walk through the prison lasted forever. The jeers, the threatening looks, and cat calls all created an unnerving feeling. I immediately realized how quickly my life changed.

Our cell was a sixteen-man cell and already contained fourteen inmates. I was dropped there with one of the new prisoners. The other fourteen had not been there long and we made friends quickly. Sadly, those friendships all had hidden costs attached. The stories are true; people offer protection, others offer drugs and still others have an affectionate level of friendship to offer. Shortly after all introductions were made, it was time for the lights to go out. Reality set in very quickly. Outside the window in our cell you could see the gun tower manned by a guard with a shotgun.

As darkness settled in, I heard a sound I will never forget - the guard pumping the shotgun with a live shell now in the chamber. As I closed my eyes, the reality of the way I had been living my life set in. I had always focused on the party; I lived without boundaries, I made bad decisions, and I had run full speed away from God and my family. All I remember from the moments before I fell asleep was asking God what I had gotten myself into?

Unfortunately, God would soon answer my question and I would find out exactly what I was up against.

I was soon to find out.

CHAPTER 6
DO YOU HEAR ME YET?

I find it amazing that in thirty-eight years of life and all the conse-quences along the way, my first night in prison was when reality set in for the first time.

That first night in prison made my situation very real. After the lights went out, there was a lot of chatter in the cell. Some of the conversations were centered around the crimes others had committed. Other conversations included guys still proclaiming their innocence. One thing I heard from several guys was how they were looking forward to visitation and how they missed family and friends. Others spoke of how, when their time was served they would straighten out. Sadly, some spoke of how they would not get caught next time, how the people that got them caught would pay for it. Still others were looking forward to a big drug, alcohol, and sex filled celebration. Mixed in with all the conversations were a couple of quiet sobs from an eighteen-year-old who was looking at a twenty-year prison term for being with the wrong people, at the wrong time, and a person died.

That night was the longest night of my life. The impact of all my bad choices, rejection of the values my parents had tried to instill in me were now upon me. My future was no longer in my hands. After what seemed to be an eternity, I did manage some sleep. It was not restful though.

The processing and orientation into the prison system was nothing at all like I thought it would be. There were tests: person-ality and IQ included. As the results of these were analyzed, they then referred us to counselors.

At the same time, we were informed that within a three-week period we would be moved to a prison where we would each have the best possibility of being reconciled to living life as a productive member of society again.

My counseling sessions went well; my counselor got my attention very quickly when he told me that my maximum "out date" was 2011. My mind turned into calculator once again. I did the math, which added up to a total of twenty years behind bars. I heard a voice say very loudly, "Do you hear me yet?"

I was speechless and overwhelmed by the news. My counselor followed it up by informing me that there were only a handful of inmates with an IQ as high as mine and that my personality tests did not suggest my type should end up in prison. I don't know if that was said to make me feel worse or to encourage me. At that moment, I was caught in the middle and not sure what to do next. The worst part was I did not know who to talk to.

Over the years many people had promised to be there for me no matter what. In the three weeks at Hoke Correctional, I had six days I could receive visitors. One friend visited once, and my father visited twice. My friend had only come to tell me not to call or count on her for anything else. She announced it was over with us.

The visit with my father was tough. His oldest son, named after his father, was in prison. For the first time, I was concerned about the feelings of someone other than myself. I watched my father get frisked, and the package he brought me searched. The image I had of my dad changed that day. He spoke to me as a friend who was concerned for me. The package he brought me held a Bible.

I was having an examination of my own beliefs and motives. For the first time in twenty years I was free from the influence of drugs, alcohol, and the need to always have another person there to complete me. As I continued to meet with my prison counselor, I found myself listening not only to the counselor, I heard what I was saying as well. Thinking about some of the things that I had experienced in my past truly astonishes me, and not in a favorable way.

As I spoke of my life, it seemed as if I shifted into the third person. I told of instances of violence, using a weapon to achieve a desired outcome, lying, cheating, and betrayal of many who got anywhere close to me. I was being honest with myself for the first time in my life. Honesty is a very big word. Being honest can bring hurt, and at the same time take it away. Only in honesty can we see who we are and in that honesty, see what God sees when He sees us.

Each night I heard the guards pump their shot guns, and a level of fear settled in and it wasn't just based on my physical surroundings. The fear I experienced was based on the reality of how far I was away from God and His plans for my life. Maybe fear would enable me to hear, maybe listen to some voices that could direct my life in a direction of hope for better days.

Time went by very quickly at Hoke Correctional. I witnessed a side of life that many only hear stories about. There were many inmates that were kept in areas away from others. There were plenty of inmates that had mastered that art of the con. As the days turned into weeks and the prospect of moving to another prison was getting closer, my challenge was to stay out of trouble, stay safe and be very careful who I said what to. Anything I said could come back to hurt me or even friends and family outside the walls of the prison.

During those days, I was challenged by my counselor with one question, "What are you willing to do?" Too often in life we are identified as we do only as we want. When we look at what we are willing to do, there very well may be a sacrifice included.

In the title of this chapter, "Do you hear me yet?" the implication is that there is someone to hear. In my life, for whatever the reason may have been, I just did not hear. Maybe I was just looking for answers in the wrong places. Maybe I was not looking or listening, maybe I was just on cruise control. One thing I became more aware of in the three weeks at Hoke County, was I wanted out of there. The reality of prison life spared no one.

Friday, July 10, 1992 did not arrive nearly fast enough. Friday was transport day in the North Carolina Department of Corrections. Part of the agreement for my plea bargain in court was for me to do my time in the Wilmington Prison Unit of the Department of Corrections 025. There were several reasons for this, first and foremost, it was close to home and more convenient for visits. The unit was also a very minimum-security unit. It was a very safe prison as most inmates there were close to the gate and did not have a lot of time remaining on their sentence. Guys close to the gate tended to be better behaved and did not want anything to slow down their release or parole.

I knew several guys in that prison too, which was a good thing. The old saying, "There is safety in numbers," is very true in prison life. Upon arriving at the unit, I had more counseling to make sure I was in the proper program, to prepare for my integration back into society again, and then I received my dormitory placement. My dorm placement was as good as I could have hoped for. It was barracks type living, it was clean and the guys in there mostly well behaved. We had two lounges with phones and televisions, clean clothes, prison uniforms two days a week, three full meals a day, and a canteen we could buy drinks, snacks and personal items from. We were outside most of each day. We lifted weights and played a lot of volleyball and basketball.

My counseling program started quickly upon my arrival. I was in the Drug Alcohol Rehabilitation Training (DART). It was a very intense program that lasted for ten hours a day for twenty-eight days. The first few days were filled with exercises that made us look utterly ridiculous. None of the thirty inmates in the class were spared any embarrassment and no areas of our lives were out of bounds for the exercise. When my hour of ridicule ended, the counselor informed me that ninety-six percent of those in the program would return to prison. His approach worked. He made me very angry and an argument ensued; he had made his point very clear. I'm not sure if I convinced him or not that day. I made up my mind though. When I got out prison, I would not be in the ninety-six percent of those who returned. That commitment I have kept.

The object of DART was to have all those attending believe that drugs or drinking was at the root of all our troubles. In an honest view of my past, I had to agree. What I began to learn is if we are willing to listen, maybe we can hear and learn. Our day at DART started at eight in the morning. We had a morning break at ten for fifteen minutes. Lunch was at noon every day and we had thirty minutes to eat. Then, we had an afternoon break for fifteen minutes, and class ended at six.

About half way through the program, we were out for an afternoon break one day when I noticed a car that looked just like moms drive by the prison very slowly. It came back by again and it was my mother. Mom was not familiar with prison protocol and pulled right up to the fence and honked. She very quickly drew a crowd of guards. My mom was a very sweet lady. Mom was taken in to the warden's office to speak with him. My mom explained she had not seen me in several months and was not aware of the rules. She offered to give the warden the pecan pie she had made and brought to give to me for her transgressions. He promptly granted her a mid-week special visit.

My mom and I had a very emotional conversation. She spoke to me in a motherly tone, and somewhat questioned me. She said, "Eugene, you have had everything you could ever ask for, restaurants, homes, possessions. What more could you possibly want?"

I responded quickly that I wanted a wife, a family, and a home. I wanted things that couldn't be taken from me. Without thinking for a moment my mother responded to me, "Matthew 6:33, 'But seek first His Kingdom and His righteousness and all these things will be added to you as well.'" I heard what she said to me. Our visit ended very shortly after that, but the impact of that scripture began to shape and motivate my life from that point forward.

After I completed the DART program, I was assigned a prison job. I left every morning with a crew to work maintenance and custodial duties on the USS North Carolina Battleship. It was a paying job with retirement type earnings of fifty cents a day. Two dollars and fifty cents a week went a long way in the prison canteen. Life was not very dramatic during those first few months. It really does define the phrase "doing time."

The routine was just that— a routine. I worked, lifted weights, played volleyball, ate and slept during the week, and then had the weekend off. The weekends usually included a visit from my dad. I also had a pastor that took interest in me and came by once a month. Pastor Cary was a constant in encouraging me that my prison sentence was not a death to my future sentence.

I started to attend church every Sunday morning in prison. There was an alternative motive for inmates who attended church services. Generally, whoever came to preach would bring some women with them. For guys who didn't experience female company while in prison, that was an added attraction.

Sunday September 27, 1992 would be the day I heard the message that God used to reach my heart and through it, changed my life. Pastor Dale Miller came to speak that Sunday morning and God got my full attention. The message was, Jesus wants to be your Lord and Savior. The scripture is Luke 2:11, "Today in the town of David a Savior has been born to you; He is Christ the Lord." Something clicked, I heard something in my heart I had never heard before. Many people that run from Jesus, leave Him hanging on the cross, suffering and bleeding, allowing His blood to continue to cover our sins. That is Jesus as Savior. The reality of our faith is that Jesus was taken off the Cross, placed in a tomb, and rose again. When we personally take Jesus off the Cross, He is risen, His Holy Spirit living within us produces His Lordship in our lives. When we submit to His Lordship, He produces His righteousness in our lives.

At thirty-eight years old I began to not only hear the Lord's message to me, I began to understand what it meant. Even though I was incarcerated, that was what it took for me to understand, outside of God, life has many voids. Recognition of emptiness in life is motivation to fill those areas that are empty. It occurs to me that we all have areas of emptiness in life. The way we deal with the emptiness determines much. From a retrospective analysis on my part, much of my life, I made those empty areas numb. There are many numbing agents out there: sex, drugs, money, alcohol, avoidance, justification, rationalization, double mindedness, apathy, procrastination. Choose one, or more— I did. None of those mindsets are conducive to hearing the Lord. In hearing the Lord, we are also recognizing that He is the Lord.

Suddenly, a light, not just in my mind also in my heart, clicked on. I got it, God had and still has a plan for my life. Everything else I tried was outside of His will for me and He could not bless me.

After all those years of being raised in a godly home, Bible teaching in Fredrick Military Academy, going to Gardner-Webb College to go into ministry, I never heard what I was listening to. It was all just sounds. There was a message attached and it took me losing everything, hitting the bottom, and ending up in prison, to be in a place where God could speak to me. The message was clear, He had never gone anywhere, I had gone places He could not bless. The last place I would ever have thought of having a real encounter of the God kind was in prison. On the night of Sunday, September 27, 1992, when God asked;

Do you hear Me yet?

Very tearfully I answered, "Yes Lord."

CHAPTER 7
JESUS IS MORE THAN SAVIOR – HE IS LORD!

The message of Jesus is desiring to be more than just my Savior. The realization that he also desired to be the Lord of my life was finally sinking in. During the next two weeks of prison life, things stirred within my heart. Still being in prison, I was troubled with my surroundings, but I was also experiencing a peace that had not been present in my life for many years. Avenues I had taken in search of peace had become distant thoughts and memories. The peace, love, and Woodstock mindset was not first and foremost any longer. The very real encounter I had with God on September 27, 1992 had taken hold of my heart and I had no choice but to hear God. The presence of God in my life, which was a result of the Gospel message I heard, had taken hold of me. As Paul spoke to the Philippians recorded in Philippians 4:7, "And the peace of God which transcends all understanding will guard your hearts and minds in Christ Jesus." Even as I could not understand it, the word of God was beginning to become alive for me. After so many years of running and ignoring God, I was hearing Him loud and clear.

Life presents so many options for us to seek peace and happiness. The reality for many of us is that peace is found in escapism. When, we are confronted with choices, we tend to choose the path of least resistance. While the path of least resistance may seem to be the easy way out, it may not be in accordance with God's plan.

My security was the death and resurrection of Jesus Christ and that in my last breath I could plead for forgiveness of my sins through his blood that was shed for me. Romans 6:1-2 states, "What shall we say, then? Shall we go on sinning so that grace may increase? By no means, we died to sin; how can we live in it any longer?" Modern churches growth focuses on grace. The grace of God becoming more alive on our lives should be the influence to lead us more into Godly lifestyles.

Sitting in prison and around all the people with so many different views on life made it very tough to focus on and participate with the work that God was doing in my life. I was at this point in my life, because of the many years of not participating with God. All along the way, God was sending me signs to slow down and seek Him. God was indeed now working within me. The days seemed to drag by as God was at work preparing me to move more into Him.

On October 9, 1992, a guard woke me up very early. This was not something I was prepared for as Fridays were transport days in the prison system. The guard that woke me informed me to pack my bags. Before he could finish speaking to me, I cut him off. I informed the guard that I was not going anywhere, my agreement was that I was going to serve my entire sentence at the prison in Wilmington, North Carolina.

To this he responded, your parole officer is here to take you home. I didn't understand. My maximum time to release was 2011, but prisons were overcrowded. Since I was considered a minimum risk for reoffending, I was eligible for early release. Words cannot accurately describe the feelings I had. After nine months of incarceration, freedom suddenly stared me in the face.

My parole officer took me to an apartment and we spent several hours discussing my full list of restrictions including boundaries and an explanation of my responsibilities. My friends had agreed to let me stay with them until my life had a more stable order.

After a couple of hours settling in to my freedom, I called my father. We exchanged greetings and I shared my good news with him. Before I could speak any further, my dad cut me off. His words to me were stern yet loving as he spoke, "Son, I do not want any more promises. I want to see it in your life." These words have remained a constant reminder for me even as a pastor. I can preach a better sermon with my life than I can with my lips.

After a very fast weekend, which included church, two friends, AL Lanier and Misha Sampson arranged a meeting with a pastor. They took me to Pastor Steve Mattis' office. We exchanged greetings with some brief discussions as to my recent past. Steve shared the grace of God with me. The more he spoke, the more I wanted to hear. For much of my life, my impression of God was based on judgement and the wrath of God toward those not walking with Him. I was now hearing God's grace poured out in the life of Jesus. God wanted me to feel His love through a proper relationship with Him, which included forgiving my sins.

When I accepted His forgiveness, the devil instantly magnified my guilt to the point where I couldn't ignore it. I began to realize all the hurt, pain and sorrow that my life inflicted on those close to me and others that I was around. Selling the drugs, the hurt of misplaced trust, those I abused in so many ways for so many years

Jeremiah 31:34 says, "For I will forgive their wickedness, and will remember their sins no more." The question for me was, If God forgave me, who am I not to forgive myself? Personal unforgiveness allowed me to set myself above what Jesus did for me on the cross. Reaching a point of totally forgiving myself is a process, and in my personal experience took time. The message of grace must saturate our lives, not only in how we deal with others but also how we deal with ourselves.

My life on parole became a daily process of service. I had to complete four hundred and eighty hours of community service as part of this process and I was placed as a school tutor in an impoverished housing project. I spent two hours a day, five days a week tutoring kids until the hours were completed. The children I worked with had many challenges. Most of them had a mother. Some had fathers in prison, and the most common bond was poverty. After all the years I had wasted, here I was with so many people that had so little; it was a major reality check for me. As God continued working to change my heart, I began to feel a deep level of compassion, even for those that tested me in every way possible.

Employment was another piece of my parole requirements that I was responsible to uphold. My reputation created a bit of a challenge, but I kept my eyes and ears open for any job openings that I may be qualified for. The first one, I applied for was a family owned and operated homestyle cooking restaurant. They had a good reputation, including Christian owned and great food. After completing the application, they interviewed me immediately and offered me the job. They explained they knew a bit about my past. I couldn't understand why they still wanted to hire me. They replied, however, by saying, "You served your sentence, it is time to live and be productive again."

This job had a very humbling aspect to it, there was an open view into the kitchen. This was a busy restaurant and many who frequented there, I knew. This humbling was necessary. Have you ever seen a chef that considered himself as one the best be humbled?

I continued to struggle and there were times when I fell. I didn't fall back into previous addiction, but just in to times of not living totally under the Lordship of Jesus Christ. The combination of job, parole and the desire of my heart to do well did lead me in a path of getting my life in order. Many of my Christian friends continued to check on me as well, and I held on to the message of grace even when I struggled.

My freedom influenced my choices. Paul states in 1 Corinthians 6:12, "Everything is permissible for me – but not everything is beneficial. Everything is permissible for me, but I will not be mastered by anything." Thinking everything is permissible is dangerous. So often it can lead to ungodly compromise. Our actions, even though permissible, may well have a negative impact on others. There were several Christians I was in relationship with during this time that participated in lifestyles that created a thought pattern in me that allowed me to sin in several areas.

I was counting on God's grace to continue to cover my sins. 1 Peter 4:8 states, "Above all, love each other deeply, because love covers a multitude of sin." Many would take advantage of grace, when in fact our deep love for God transfers our thoughts to impact our behavior in a way it is beneficial to others. As we claim Christianity, do we think about what is good for us, what we are entitled to, or do we model Christ in a manner we are serving what is best for others? From a personal view, are my permitted behaviors a good witness for anyone that is watching me, who may be struggling in their own lives with the same thing as I, as a Christian, am doing?

This season in my life was a time of transforming my emotions, my convictions and taking a very deep look at my faith. Looking deeply at faith requires an honest look at how that faith lines up with the totality of biblical truth. I personally found that holding on to several favorite passages in one sense or another gave me entitlement to brush certain character issues under the carpet.

As Christians, it is important to realize when we are truly born again, the old person of our past dies. The perception that the act of baptism seals our salvation is a bit flawed. In John chapter three, Jesus speaks to a Nicodemus, who questions Him about eternal salvation. In John 3:3 Jesus says, "I tell you the truth, no one can see the Kingdom of God unless he is born again." For many of us, this can be a challenging statement. How can we possibly be born again? In John 3:5-6 He continues to explain, "Jesus answered, I tell you the truth, no one can enter the kingdom of God unless he is born of water and the Spirit. Flesh gives birth to flesh, but the Spirit gives birth to spirit." Jesus surprised Nicodemus with His response. The encouragement here was that Pharisees and other religious leaders must be truly born again in spirit. It was not just an act to be seen by men, but was meant to be an inner transformation of spirit. Born again means the Holy Spirit dwells within us.

There were so many areas in my life where I, needed God's guidance. For too many years my life was guided by a mentality of immediate gratification, little thought, and even less truth. My current state had me questioning what truth really is and how would I know for sure if it is truth? It became obvious how much I needed to learn. Through strong influence from others that were close to me and cared about my well-being, I started searching God's word.

In John 16:12-13 Jesus says, "I have so much more to you, more than you can now bear. But when He, the Spirit of truth comes, He will guide you into all truth. He will not speak on His own; He will speak only what He hears, and He will tell you what is yet to come."

The Spirit guides those seeking to be true followers of Jesus in truth. The Holy Spirit reveals truth as we can understand it. This takes a person seeking with a mind set on learning the truth of God. More than you can now bear challenged me. There are times we may not be ready as we can still try to compromise or may not be willing to understand. What in my life limited my capacity to understand and embrace truth, according to God's indwelling Spirit. The question caused me to take a deeper look into my character.

God had a plan for me. I needed to be in a place spiritually for Him to reveal it to me. I needed that revelation to become reality in order to continue to focus on my new life that is God centered. I had to remain to be committed to new truth, the old me was history. God was creating a new me with eternal values. The season of understanding the sacrifice for my atonement and salvation was here.

I was earnestly seeking the truth, the revealing of God's plan for me. The revelation of God's truth for me was freeing me from the bondage of the knowledge that led to my past. It wasn't a judge or jury determining my fate any longer. It was an active presence of God through His Holy Spirit indwelling me that spoke the truth to me. God was bringing His words that I heard on a dark side street in Charleston, South Carolina as a gun was held to my head, "I have plans for you!"

Yes, He does have a plan for me, He has plans for me, just as He does for you. The truth is now, God pursues those He loves, He loves us all. In that love there is correction that leads to truly being born again. Being born again creates desire for more of Him.

Yes Lord, I hear you, I do want more. I want Jesus to be alive and active in my life, I need your Lordship.

My encouragement to each reading these words, speak them out loud and don't just hope for an answer, expect Him to answer how He can indeed lead your life.

CHAPTER 8
SEE YE FIRST – HIM

Looking back to when I was in prison and the day my mother came and first visited me, I remembered the scripture verse she shared with me. Matthew 6:33, "But seek first His Kingdom and His righteousness and all these things will be given to you as well." My initial thoughts about the promise of this verse were a bit out of order. The first thoughts about these things being given to me, was my regaining all that I had lost.

My immediate thoughts about "these things will be given to you" focused on me. This is where our seeking in life must take on a new perspective. To shift the priorities that define our search, we must first have a better understanding of the Lord, which in turn leads to better understanding of the truth.

When life is lived in a very temporary manner, it seems that reality of spiritual knowledge escapes us. We lack perception of anything that has a lasting value. I think that in this place in life we lack the ability to grasp the attributes of righteousness and living in a manner that the Kingdom of Heaven has no influence.

The reality is, that in this place mentally, we are lost. If we are lost, we really have no idea where we are and quite possibly go in many wrong directions in our search for the truth. In that line of thought, do I search as fervently for the unknown as I do for a set of lost keys? Once I have found my keys, my car has value to me. The same can be applied to searching fervently for Biblical truth. Once I have knowledge of God's truth, it does in fact have more value in my life.

When we change our motivation in this life to our eternal life, there are many encouragements in God's Word that act as the key to unlocking our ability to get there. Looking at this as an objective in light of this verse, the key is living a righteous life in God's eyes. Righteousness is defined as behavior that is morally justifiable or right. Coming from a life that was seriously lacking in moral integrity, this posed a major challenge. The style of my life, the constant altered state of consciousness, pleasing myself and just going with the flow, lacked morality.

While I had decided to be a totally different person and live a life that was pleasing to God, this was going to be a challenge. To make the decision was a lot easier to do that in fact doing it. I was working, paying my debt to society, and when possible attending church. We had a great pastor, great worship and great people. It did in fact take more from me to achieve the outcome the Lord had for me.

I felt my priorities were coming into an order which had been missing in my life. I had my aims in life, surfing when there were waves, fishing when the opportunity arose, and the search for the perfect woman with whom to spend the rest of my life. The truth is, when I decided to seek Jesus, the devil tried very hard to distract me in any way he could.

A year after being out of prison, was a time when my mind was set on not making the same mistakes that would send me back there. Seeking first righteousness did at times take a hit. When I made mistakes, like a few too many drinks when I was playing darts, an overwhelming guilt would consume me. John 16:8, became very true," When He comes, He will convict the world of guilt in regard to sin, righteousness and judgement."

Not sure I was prepared to have a conscience. It seems that when I opened my heart to the Lord, He took me seriously. I had a great job, a home, plenty of incentive to stay out of jail. I did still compromise my behavior at times. We kept a radio in the kitchen where I was working. During the early spring of 1994 a local station had a call-in contest to win tickets to the ACC tournament in Charlotte, North Carolina. The prize included accommodation and tickets to the event. I called in and won. As part of my parole, I had to get permission from my parole officer to go out of town. During my visit, she surprised me with a urine test for drugs. I still had a problem with smoking pot, I failed the test and it cost me the ability to go on the trip with her permission. This was a four-day tournament. I had a friend that purchased the tickets for the first two days, which left two days. At a considerable risk I decided to go for the final two days. I thank God that I did not get caught. I shared this to say, as good as I thought I was doing, there was still a lot of work to be done in my personal life. My initial thoughts that by following Jesus, my life would just automatically get easier wasn't real.

Yes, following Jesus is the ideal for our eternal well-being, it is filled with much discipline and sacrifice in the here and now. After so many years of living a life separated from the will of God, it was difficult to stay away from those lifestyles that had me ensnared. To submit to the Lordship of Jesus and be born again meant a total makeover of who I was. This brought me to a point of realizing, I did not know who I was. The Lordship and knowing who Jesus was, was the beginning of the knowledge of who God had planned for me to be. That is in fact the reality of each of our lives. This is where the convicting work of the Holy Spirit began to identify the sin in my life. I felt as though I had come so far in three years since prison, yet I wasn't where God was leading me yet. The attitude of my heart was softening, and the acceptance of my shortcomings were now replacing the denial and justification of my actions. The right relationship with God involves more than just telling people that you are a Christian and going to church on Sunday.

I needed to take a total personal inventory of the life I was living since I was released. I was still depending on personal strength and determination to change. This held me back. I had an encounter with the Lord, He was pursuing me for His plan in my life. I had to move into the place of total trust in Him, where I was weak, He desired to be strong. He wanted me to seek Him. When we attempt to live life according to the standards of this world, trust can be a very big issue.

My relationship with my family had greatly improved over this period. My mom was still very concerned about my relationships with women. I went to church with my parents occasionally and that was encouraging for them. They did not approve of my weekend trips away with women and activities that God could not bless. My immediate response was generally to argue, it was an argument that I could not win. Mom always had scripture to share and on one occasion she shared a scripture where Paul was speaking to Timothy.

Timothy 1:12 states: "That is why I am suffering as I am. Yet I am not ashamed, because I know whom I believed, and am convinced that He is able to guard what I have entrusted to Him for that day."

This learning process was more than I had figured on. My feelings of guilt were based on my consciousness of sin in my life. These feelings were based on God's presence in my life, convicting me of areas that He could not bless, this was not condemnations. I was beginning to learn, the devil really wanted me to feel condemnation in conviction. God out of His great love for us, convicts us of our sin, so that there is proper relationship with Him, which leads to no condemnation for us as we live now in Christ.

I was living with a friend during this period in my life and working two jobs. Both jobs were as a chef. Since my life was still a financial mess, my mode of transportation was a bike. The two restaurants were about five miles away from where I lived, in opposite directions. Spending so much time on my bike, I had plenty of time to talk to the Lord. What He started revealing to me, He already knew what I wanted to say and that I needed to learn to listen for His voice. I was having a hard time trying to understand all that He was saying to me. What I did hear and realize, I could not receive all that He had for me as I still had one part of my life seeking the pleasures of this world. Worship, prayer and hearing God's Word always had a way of drawing me into a place where my thoughts and feelings were at peace. I was beginning to trust my feelings as they were influenced by a greater awareness of what the presence of the Lord brought into my life.

The summer of 1994 was a time when I was very active physically. I was fishing, eating plenty of good fish, surfing, playing softball and hanging with friends. Sadly, all this activity resulted in me drifting away from God, the church and my friends in the church. During one visit with my mom, her discernment was overwhelming, she shared another verse with me. 1 Corinthians 15:33-34," Do not be misled, bad company corrupts good character. Come back to your senses as you ought and stop sinning; for there are some who are ignorant of God, I say this to your shame." God spoke to me directly through my mom in this moment. The word character struck a nerve. God did not just want lip service from me in an environment full of friends. He wanted my whole heart. He knew that would produce the necessary change in my character to be pleasing to him. When the change in a person's character is Godly, then our true pursuit of righteousness can begin. My life still resembled that of any other

sinner. I was hoping for an outpouring of grace to cover my sins. I was still in the process of working on submitting to His Lordship in my life. In this learning curve in my life God presented me with some very undeniable signs, a major sign was coming very unexpectedly.

On the Saturday morning of Labor Day weekend, I strolled across the parking lot at work and in the distance, I saw a man, not clearly, but I thought I knew him and I shouted a greeting in some very unchurch like language. As I got closer, it became clear, he was not who I thought he was. Instead, it was one of the pastors from the church, Steve Jensen. Very gracefully he replied, "Hello, I've missed seeing you in church."

I was embarrassed. In an attempt to smooth things over, I promised him that he would see me in church the next morning." After work, I went fishing for a while with my roommate. At home that evening as we talked, I told him of my conversation with the pastor. I told him that I wanted to get a good night's sleep so that I would get up for church the next morning. He asked me, "Why do you want to go to church?"

My response somewhat surprised me, "There are some nice girls in church and it is probably the best place to find a wife." Little did I know, the next day I would meet my wife.

I saw the same pastor when I arrived at church the next day. He greeted me warmly and chuckled a bit as I stumbled through trying to explain my colorful greeting of the day before. The morning service had special guests from New Zealand. I paid very close attention as they spoke—mainly so I could understand them. The message was clear though, they had a passion for God that impacted them very deeply. This passion led them around the world to share the love of God.

After the service, a guy I knew, came up to talk to me. After saying hello, he asked if I was still riding my bike a lot. He went on to say there was a girl at church who had just purchased a new bike. She was looking for someone to ride with because she was not a local and was not comfortable riding alone. With no real thought, I agreed to ride with her. After all, since she was not local, she didn't know me or my checkered past.

Within a couple of minutes, he came back up to me with a younger, attractive woman. Before my mind could go totally crazy, she said, "Hello."

I was stunned, not that she had said hello, but that she had the same accent as the folks from the New Zealand group. That was the day that I met Shelley. After chatting for a few minutes, we agreed to ride bikes the next day.

The surprises continued as Sam, the guy who introduced us, came back to see if we wanted to go to lunch with a crowd of other singles. It only took a minute for us to look at each other and say yes. Shelley and I sat beside each other at lunch and continued to get acquainted.

When lunch was almost over, a guy sitting across the table from us asked, "How long have you guys been married?" We looked at each other and then back at him, and responded pretty much in unison; "we just met."

Early the next afternoon, Shelley showed up with her new bike, hooked on the back of her car. Shortly after, we left on about a thirty-mile ride. As we rode, at one point, Shelley became distracted, hit the edge of the pavement and fell off her bike and banged her knee. With no big fuss, she wiped the blood off and was ready to continue the ride. I was impressed!

We rode down to the point on Wrightsville Beach. Shelley had come to America a couple of years earlier as a travelling Occupational Therapist. She worked thirteen-week contracts and saw a lot of the country. In between contracts, she would travel. She had come to Wilmington before the start of a new contact and had visited the Vineyard, the church we met in. She had left for a trip overseas and the Sunday we met she had not been there for a while. As the ride turned back toward home, we stopped at the restaurant I worked at for a snack on the deck. This was a very nice restaurant located on the Intercoastal Waterway. As we sat and talked about our lives, where we had been, our families, our countries and so much more, I am not sure either of us were aware of how dramatically a chance meeting in church would change the course of our lives.

As the day came to an end, we agreed that a bike ride the next day would be enjoyable. During our second ride, we talked much more and stopped to have dinner together, this led to a much deeper conversation. I shared with her concerning my past and that I had been previously married. We talked for a long time that night. We left the restaurant to ride our bikes back to my house. As we said, "Good night", I sensed we had both reached out to each other. We learned that we were both committed to going ahead in life in a manner that God could bless.

I did not fall asleep easily that night, God continued to remind me that His plans were still in place. He helped me to remember my visit with my Mom while I was still in prison. My mother had asked, "Eugene, what do you want out of life?" My immediate response was, "a wife, a home, a family, things that can't be taken away from me."

Even in my flawed state of seeking Him first, could He be honoring the desire of my heart? Shelley and I continued to ride bikes and go to church together. We prayed together, and we joined a small group of other young Christians. Neither one of us knew what was next. Her work contract would end soon, and she was meant to be moving back towards Washington state.

We both put all our faith and trust in God pertaining to our relationship.

CHAPTER 9
YOU JUST GOT TO BELIEVE

I had mixed feelings while embarking on this part of my journey. So many times, in my past there had been seasons of security which brought me stability. I am sure many of us can identify with that internal questioning, based on past life experiences; how long until it all falls over again? This is the place where the proverbial rubber hits the road. Yes, it was time for me to get real with my faith. My personal biblical challenge came from Hebrews 11:6, "And without faith it is impossible to please God, because anyone that comes to Him, must believe that He exists and that He rewards those who earnestly seek Him." Sounded like a good plan to me. We can all have those moments that sound like the perfect plan, the key is putting that plan in action.

My immediate plan was very predictable. At forty years old, my clock was ticking regarding having a wife, a home and a family. It seemed the logical course of action for me was to pursue getting to know Shelley. After all, she was a very attractive lady, Christian and on the surface seemed interested in me. Things were looking good. I had a good job, was staying out of trouble, having good visits with my parole officer. My relationship with my parents was being restored.

During this season in life our extended family suffered a terrible loss. A cousin of mine, with a troubled history like mine, decided to take his own life. He had lived close to us, and had always been like a brother to me and seemed to be a happy person. Hearing the news shook us all. It also brought concern for me within our family, because of our similar history. I was living forty-five minutes from my parents at the time. My father made the drive for a visit, to talk to me about my cousin's suicide. As we talked, my father got very emotional. I will always remember the words Dad used. He spoke to me in such a sad, but encouraging manner. "Eugene", he said, "You have had a very tough life to this point, please tell me this is not an option for you." The impact of those words went deep. For a moment, it suddenly dawned on me how my life and choices had so impacted those close to me. At forty years old, I realized how deeply my father and mother loved me and were genuinely concerned for me. Some things about my life that I never took much time to think about, were becoming reality. I had always been so busy thinking about me, that I did not think about the negative impact of my life actions. These actions did concern others, especially those closest to me. As reassuringly as possible, I answered my Dad, "No matter how bad anything has ever been in my life, suicide has never been an option." We both were overcome with the emotions of the moment, and cried. My father hugged me, that made me cry more. Suddenly, the flood of emotions allowed me to realize that no matter the mistakes, failures of my past; those I had hurt the most still loved me. For so long in my life, love had some very distorted meanings to me. I had substituted many one-night stands, short term relationships, drugs, alcohol and even violence to replace my need for true love. The immediate realization of my father's love for me brought me face to face with the fact of how deeply my Father God loves even me, so much. 1 John 2:1-2, "My dear children, I write this to you so that you will not sin. But if anybody does sin, we have one who speaks to the Father in our defense – Jesus Christ, the Righteous One. He is the atoning sacrifice for our sins, and not only for ours but also for the sins of the whole world." God was speaking to me directly in this passage I heard "My dear child."

I hope those reading this will hear, no matter where you have been, no matter what you have done, God holds you in very high regard as His dear child. Make this message personal, He gave Jesus for you!

I now was at the place in my life of choosing to believe not just in God; I now was in the place to believe in His love for me. The measure of love is based on our real experiential knowledge of His love to us each, His personal love. It is not to say that I perfected this love thing, it is to say, I believe in it and I needed more of it in my life. That moment, with my father, opened my life up to pursuing what I now realized was the true meaning of love. This was the moment – move on it!

Now, back to Shelley. Here was a woman that God had placed in my life. Am I going to yield to personal doubts as to my ability to be cared for and loved by a woman or trust God to lead me into a relationship He had for me?

You always count on family to be there right when you need them. My brother, David, was playing softball in Wilmington one evening and this was the perfect occasion for Shelley to meet a member of the family. The introduction was made and conversation started. Upon hearing Shelley's distinct accent and finding out she was from New Zealand, David asked what was their favorite fish for their famous fish-n-chips. Without hesitation Shelley answered. "Groper". My brother being rather quick witted responded by saying, "You have found one here." Took a moment for that response to sink in for Shelley, this was followed by her blushing and my brother laughing. With a very Kiwi accent grouper comes out sounding like groper. This exchange prompted a great deal of thought in her future responses, especially when David was present.

On another occasion when Shelley and I were visiting the riverfront in Southport, we saw my sister Mary and a boyfriend of hers. The introductions were made and Mary noted what a good thing it was for Shelley to be from so far away, she did not have the benefit of knowing my rather colorful past.

Shelley took it thankfully as it was spoken, in good humor.

As Shelley survived the initial meetings with my family, we began to feel more comfortable seeing where God was leading us. We both seemed to sense how important our Christian relationship was. Both of us had very different backgrounds. With Shelley being from the other side of the world, even though we spoke the same language, many words had different meanings and cultural ideals were somewhat different as well.

Shelley and I were pursuing having a Christian relationship and there were several things we agreed to. We read the Bible together, spoke about what we read and prayed together. We also found the importance of spending time with other Christians. We saw similar Christians, like us, that were real people, loving the real Jesus and living in the real world. This was the motto of our church.

Our relationship was very young at this stage, we had been seeing each other for just two months. As we began to know more about each other the closer we grew in our relationship. Since we both shared in the memories of past bad relationships, we both had cautions and concerns about moving forward. Shelley was working thirteen-week contract, and her current contract started September 1994 and would end the last week of November 1994. She had already been told her new contract would move her back towards the west coast of America. We both saw this as a time to make a decision. It brought us to a place we knew we loved each other in a manner we had not experienced with any other before. Our choices

were to have a long-distance relationship, and this would be tough; end our relationship, even tougher and painful; or commit to each other in getting engaged and trust God to handle the rest. On Saturday, November 19, 1994, I asked Shelley to marry me, she said, "Yes."

Have you ever been in that moment that was very real, yet it seemed you were detached from the reality of the moment? The flood of emotions was mixed with the shock of a person saying yes to spending a life together, then there was an event to plan. Shelley and I were still wondering how this was all going to work. We set the date for the wedding to be February 4, 1995, and started praying harder. Thanksgiving was the week following the engagement. This was the perfect time to announce our plans to our family and friends. We planned to have Thanksgiving dinner at the condo that Shelley was renting. This was Shelley's first Thanksgiving because in New Zealand they did not celebrate Thanksgiving.

Being the chef for many family functions, the food for this occasion was my responsibility. No true Southerner is going to have a Thanksgiving feast without a mess of collard greens. Shelley knew very little about collards. Her job was to ride about forty-five minutes into rural, very country North Carolina to find the roadside stands that sold the collards. She had seen them in the stands, and volunteered to buy some fresh collards to cook. I suggested that she purchase two heads of collards and that should be plenty. Very proudly Shelley accomplished the mission. Upon arriving home, she opened her car trunk, and two of the largest heads of collards I had ever seen completely filled her trunk. They were great and we ate collards all winter from those two heads. She has left the responsibility for buying collard to me ever since. The dinner, complete with turkey, oyster dressing, gravy, candied yams, green rice, collards and jalapeno cheese cornbread, was great. My mother makes the best chocolate chip pecan pie and as we had our dessert, we made our announcement of the engagement. Everyone was very happy. We then shortly made a long-distance call to New Zealand and shared the news with her family, they were equally pleased.

Moving forward now, we had some plans to make. The most urgent being Shelley's contract was expiring. God was in control; her contract for the same facility was extended and that was a blessing.

Things were good, actually very good. Our circle of Christian friends was growing. My work was good, her job was secure and we were growing closer. We had many long talks. With her being a few years younger, much of our talk was of starting a family. We shared many ideas about how we desired to have children and the manner that they would be raised. There was much that we agreed on.

This may be a touchy subject for many, my desire in this book has been to be totally honest. Many Christian singles face the reality of dealing with sex outside of the bonds of marriage. We did as well and we knowing it was wrong in God's eyes gave in to

70

that desire. Shortly before Christmas we found out that we were going to have a child. With the wedding February 4th, we planned to keep the pregnancy a secret until after the wedding, which we did but felt very guilty. What would people think if they knew? With our secret safe, our desire for the Lord continued to grow. This was a tough place to be in, God just seemed to pour out extra grace on us as we were honestly trying to do things right. We had a rapidly approaching wedding.

The church we were very involved in was a Vineyard. This was a very happy, loving, grace based church. It was pastored by the man who shared the message of grace with me when I got out of prison. He wrote the forward to this book and was also going to officiate our wedding.

There was a big revival going on in Toronto, Canada. Several of our church members went to the revival and came back very different people. Not really wanting to be left out, we wanted to go. We spoke to our small group leaders and made the plans to go in mid-January 1995 with them. This revival was totally amazing. There were over ten thousand people in attendance from all over the world. The weekend we were there marked the one-year anniversary of a mighty move of God. It started in a small church with about one hundred twenty in attendance, this was the Toronto Airport Vineyard. This revival was to be from January 20-23, 1994; and continued six days a week for the next twelve and a half years.

Something profound happened to us while there, something like we had never experienced before. We joined literally thousands down front for prayer. As we approached our time to be prayed for; we noticed many people deeply touched, many tears and much of the joy of the Lord being released.

As we were prayed for, we received a word and it had to be from God. Shelley was only three months pregnant at the time and not showing at all. The man praying for us, prayed for the unborn child she was carrying. The word went further to say, we were forgiven for our transgressions as the child was conceived out of wedlock. We were both in a state of awe at how the Lord spoke directly to us. As we processed this, we knew there were people we had to ask forgiveness from as well. Going through life it is so very important to clear the air with those who we sin against in any level, ask for their forgiveness. Saying I am sorry leaves too many doors open. Are you sorry you got caught, or are you sorry you did it and just sorry they found out? Asking forgiveness is acknowledging the offense and being able to be made right in relationship.

Our lives really sped up on our return from Canada. February 4, 1995 was our wedding date and only two weeks away. All plans were made and in place. Shelley's mom and sister Debbie were set to arrive from New Zealand and the excitement was growing. My parents had chosen their favorite barbeque restaurant for our wedding rehearsal dinner, the families and wedding party had a great meal. Barbeque in America does not mean the same as in New Zealand. The food very different, it did meet my soon to be Mother-in-law's approval. In New Zealand to barbeque is just to put meat on the Barbie, down here in the southern states of America it is the process, plus our own signature sauces and so much more. We had barbeque ribs, chicken and chopped barbeque, all cooked perfectly and sauced in a manner that makes you "wanna smack yo mama," not literally, just a southern saying for good food. The hushpuppies, which New Zealanders just weren't aware such delicacies existed, were served with cole slaw, baked beans and not to be left out of any proper Southern meal, collard greens. Yep, Shelley's mom and sister got a real education on the very best vittles in Southern cuisine. The groom's cake was a great chocolate cake that my mom made from scratch. I will spare the description as I would not want to tempt anyone to chew a page out of the book in an attempt to taste it. After a couple of hours of enjoying the time of everyone getting to know each other we called it an evening. There was a big day coming – WOW!

Wedding day arrived. We were both excited and pleased the day was here. A day that just a year earlier neither one of us saw coming that quickly. All the insecurities of so many years passed very quickly when I saw the bride walking down the aisle towards me. The feeling of unconditional love and lifelong commitment became reality very fast. Our vows were exchanged, the kiss shared and we were off. I must say, in style. Several of our friends had gotten a limousine to take us the twenty-five-minute ride from the church to the restaurant on the Inter-Coastal Waterway where the reception was held. Many thanks to those guys at the Bridge Tender, where I was working. They allowed me to prepare our reception food the day earlier and then served it to us, our families and friends. It was great!

After the reception, we were off for a short honeymoon to Charleston, South Carolina. A couple of reasons for it being short, my mother-in-law and sister-in-law were still here and they chaperoned us on this trip. This was pretty cool, they weren't aware of the beauty and culture of Low Country South Carolina that is found in historical Charleston. We sampled plenty of good, fresh seafood; mainly shrimp and oysters in many styles. We also visited a couple of Civil War era plantations. I think my mother-in-law would have stayed!

Now back to life as a married couple, we were happy and feeling very blessed. There was an issue we still had to deal with. Sharing that we were expecting a child was going to cause some raised eyebrows over the timing of the pregnancy. We first shared it with family, they did the math. We assured them we married because of our love for each other first and foremost. Even in their shock, they quickly shared in our joy. We next shared with our small group, they were happy for us as well. Our group leaders that had been raising us up to be leaders did the math as well. One thing about church life we learned then and this lesson remains, there should be correction when people in the church, especially leaders, are found to have erred.

We were called in to a meeting with our leaders and the pastor that was over the small group ministries in our church. They very gracefully explained to us that it was necessary for us to step back for a while from leadership. This brought a big ouch to my pride. I responded by being defensive. We had been prayed for in Toronto and assured God had forgiven us. The truth is, we were ministering in a local church and to be submitted to the local authority. Shelley sat gracefully as I was preparing to reject this church discipline. When I opened my mouth to respond, the words, "I will not submit," did not come out. My response was very humbling as I spoke the words, "I will submit to your God given authority." It was like a giant cloud lifting and we were now freed to live for Christ, no secrets.

Church discipline and correction are the necessities of church life that are missing in many churches today. Paul writes to Titus 3:1 "Remind the people to be subject to rulers and authorities, to be obedient and to do whatever is good." We learned through this life lesson how important it is to be humble enough to submit, even if painful. God's plans are in place and as people seeking His fullest blessings, we should submit to Him and yes those He brings in our lives to lead us. The dynamic of this lesson was realizing I had not done a stellar job leading my own life.

Shelley and I had fun being married. Life was full of surprises and smiles. When we married, I had long hair and a beard. Quite impulsively, one morning I woke and decided to shave my beard. Shelley is a very sound and late sleeper when given the opportunity. I eased out of bed, not to wake her and shave my face clean. With Shelley still asleep, I climbed back in bed. A few minutes later, with her still half asleep, she rolled over and placed her arm across my shoulder with her hand close to my chin. She awoke very quickly not sure who this clean-shaven guy was in the bed next to her.

Her mother came for a visit as it was getting close to time for our first child to be born. We were sitting around the breakfast table chatting, drinking morning tea and Mum was reading the local newspaper. We noticed Mum turning a bit red and questioned if she was okay. She shared the newspaper with Shelley. There was a big advertisement in the newspaper about a shag contest, a dance popular in southeast America, with lessons following. Needless to say, shagging does not mean the same thing in New Zealand as it does in America. We all shared a good laugh.

Time was passing very quickly with the child on the way. We chose to take a real honeymoon and went to Cancun, Mexico. A great resort on the water with many activities to participate in. There just happened to be a beach volleyball game starting and I joined in. After the game, very sandy and sweaty and being from the East Coast with the Caribbean Sea right there, I made a dash into the water to rinse off. The locals we had been playing with were standing on the beach closely watching us. As we were using the water and our hands to rinse off-we both simultaneously experienced some very painful burning all over our bodies. Exiting the water, the locals shared with us that the jelly fish were spawning and that as we were rubbing the sand off we were spreading the stinging jelly. We were very recognizable as our walk made us appear to have been riding a horse for weeks. The lesson learned here, if you are ever at a beach and no one else is in the water-don't go in!

We also saw God's protection on us and our unborn child on this trip. Shelley and I decided to go parasailing, we did this tandem. What an exhilarating experience it was, thirty minutes up in the air, over the Caribbean Sea and viewing much of the Yucatan. The adventure ended with us landing gently in shallow water. The next clients where a couple of American ladies. They were strapped into the same seat we had just gotten out of. As the boat began to pull them up, about fifteen feet off ground, the rope to the seat snapped and it crashed to the ground. One of the ladies left in an ambulance. We went over and prayed with and for the lady. At the same time, we realized God's protection over us, especially our unborn child.

Time was passing very quickly now and our child was due. September 6, 1995 our little bundle of joy, Hannah Maree Tomlinson was born. God is so good. The feeling of having a desire of my life was indescribable. Shortly after the birth of our daughter, we enlisted a realtor friend of ours to find a house that met our needs and that we could afford to buy. The week before Christmas 1995 we closed on the house we really loved. What a blessing to spend our first Christmas as a family in our house.

Father /Daughter Surfing trip Stent Rd Taranaki NZ

Cruisin the South Island Harley Road trip

NZ fur seals, Kaikoura South island Harley Road trip

Lake Ferry Wairarapa North island NZ
Uncle Lews, a favorite get away

Lighthouse Annual Easter Egg hunt ,little Elizabeth in pink and me as Easter Bunny

The original Lighthouse building "This is my house claim it"

Cape fear sunrise a place of inspiration

Me preaching Southport Baptist Church

CHAPTER 10
TRAVELLING AND GROWING

I n January of 1996, it was time for Shelley's extended family to meet me and Hannah. It was my first trip to New Zealand and as the flight was long and we planned to be there for six weeks. January is the summer there and I planned to take full advantage of a break from our winter by packing two surfboards, and be ready for any surf conditions. We spent much time with her family and friends while at the same time seeing much of the country. I was blessed to see the lower North Island east coast, across the Wairarapa Ranges to Lake Ferry. This is a very rugged area where Shelley's Uncle Lou had a place. I went paua diving, fishing, surfing and hung out with the locals in very bush like campers. Paua is a favorite seafood, much like abalone. You harvest the meat and then process the shells into beautiful jewelry and artwork. This was the first of many trips to Lake Ferry, a place I really love.

 Our journey continued up the North Island to Raglan, a small, quaint coastal village made popular in the 1966 surf movie classic, The Endless Summer. Raglan is known for the longest and best breaking left in the world. In surf language, I am a goofy foot, which means I surf right foot forward and my natural direction in surfing is to go left. The surfing was great there as were the people and the food.

Shelley wanted me to experience the beauty of the South Island as well. Our trip there was on The Inter-Islander Ferry, which was a three-hour trip across the Cook strait. I had never to that point in my life witnessed so much natural beauty as the mountains that descended into the sounds, the schools of porpoises that ran beside the ferry, and the occasional flip of a whale tail. The long white clouds dancing across the sky gave a better meaning to the name Aotearoa, the land of the long white cloud. After the trip that could only be described as breath taking in its natural beauty, we arrived at the port village of Picton on the South Island and disembarked the ferry with about three hundred other cars.

The rugged, snowcapped mountain ranges, unspoiled coast line, seal colonies and small beautiful cities were the highlight of our first day travelling south. We arrived in Kaikoura for the night and we were both very happy that Hannah, now just four months old was such a wonderful travel partner. I was overwhelmed by the natural beauty of the land. We rested after a great meal of fresh local fish prepared signature Kiwi fish-n-chip style, batter fried to perfection.

The next morning, we were up and off to Christchurch. I continued to be amazed with the natural beauty of God's creation. Christchurch was a beautiful city that displayed the historical beauty of the country. We booked a train ride with Tranz Alpine, it was a full day from Christchurch through the Southern Alps to Greymouth. The trip was rated as one of the top five train trips in the world, my personal rating is the same. We cruised through valleys, over beautiful rivers and endless pastures of sheep and cattle, surrounded by majestic mountains with peaks covered with snow and touching the clouds. My mind could not comprehend all of the beauty. People who lived out there are typically disconnected from much of life as we know it. I am so thankful that God allowed me to take that trip. So many experiences on that trip that challenged me. Many times, in life we can only imagine places. When the imagination becomes reality, it allows us to better understand the beauty of what God has created and even expands our ability to anticipate our eternal home.

The physical challenges were ever present as well. Getting used to driving on the wrong side of the road, learning to navigate roundabouts, all new to me. The adjustment to January being summer and noon on Monday being the same time as six pm Sunday on the east coast of America, so much of a difference. A country so small, three million people and sixty million sheep. All of my normal was being expanded to for a brief six weeks being a new normal. I knew I would be back, not just because of Shelley's family or the adventures, there was something more, but I could not put my finger on it then.

Upon returning to America, we began looking forward to another trip to New Zealand. Our lives were very full and busy with; raising a child, church and work. God was growing us individually and as a couple. In the summer of 1996 we learned that we were expecting another child. At three months into the pregnancy, Shelley started feeling very different one day, and our worst fears were realized. We suffered a miscarriage. It was painful for the both of us. The greatest lesson out of it was, while being so involved with the community of church, there were others who had experienced the same grief. Many came around Shelley and myself during that time and ministered God's love to us in so many practical ways.

God gained a very special angel that day and we experienced His love on a much deeper level. Some hurts are much tougher to get over and we are so grateful for God's love being ever present in such times. About a year after that happened, we found out we were expecting again. There were sometimes that we were a bit shaky in our faith, but we pressed on and trusted God. On April 25, 1998 God blessed us with a very happy, healthy baby girl, Kaely. Nothing would do but to plan another trip to New Zealand to introduce our newest family member to her New Zealand family. Life was very good for us during that time. The words that I had spoken to my mother so long before, "I want a wife, a home, a family," had in fact become a reality.

As we prepared for our next trip to New Zealand in the spring of 1999, the plan was to celebrate Kaely's first birthday with her Kiwi family. There were also a couple of friends of ours that wanted to join us for part of the trip to surf, so we planned another trip to Raglan as well.

Shelley along with our two daughters, her mom and our friends, loaded the van and were off for a surf trip. Our first night we made it to Opunake to surf a well-known surf spot, Stent Road. After dinner in the local hotel and a good night's rest we were up for an early morning surf session and back on the road to Raglan. Upon arrival in Raglan, we were treated to very good surf. After a couple hours of surf, we continued our evening with dinner at The Raglan Hotel. Our dinner conversation was focused on our Christian lives. There was a table close enough to us that the folks there over-heard our conversation and the mentioning of the name, Jesus. Very politely they asked if they could join us and we were happy to say "yes". Their first question was, "who is Jesus?" We were a bit surprised by this question. How could someone not know who Jesus is? For a couple of hours, we answered their questions as best we could. We gave them a Bible we had with us that had a commentary and concordance to make their search for answers easier. We went back to the motel for the night. I was a bit restless and went out to sit by the bay to process the dinner conversation and to ask God the question, "How can people in our world not know who Jesus is?" It was very silent and peaceful when I heard a still, small voice speaks to me, "You are coming back." My immediate response was, of course I am, Shelley's family is here. God's response was quick and clear, "You are coming back to serve Me here." Not sure how it works for everyone else, for me, when God speaks, it is clear, direct and then confirmed.

The surf trip came to an end. We returned to Shelley's parents' home and celebrated Kaely's first birthday. She wore more of her cake than she ate, I am sure those pictures will come in handy at some point later in her life. It was time to prepare for our trip home, back to life in America. We could both sense God was preparing us for something new.

Not long after returning to America, the words the Lord spoke to me in Raglan were confirmed. We were back two weeks when one of our pastors asked if we would like to lead a mission trip to New Zealand. My answer was obviously, "of course."

Shortly after that conversation Shelley's grandmother died and she needed to go back to attend her funeral. With Kaely being so young she needed to travel with Shelley. With a young child and luggage, it was a bit of a struggle going from the international terminal in Auckland to the domestic terminal. A nice man offered to help Shelley with her bags and then gave her his card. He was a pastor of a church near Shelley's home. When Shelley came back to America, she gave me the pastor's card and I contacted him with the plan we had to do a mission trip there. He was more than happy to partner with us in this endeavor.

We put a team together and all the pieces were falling into place very nicely. We had a team of ten people lined up and our pastor friend had lined up two weeks' worth of places to minister, including his church.

We arrived in Auckland and our ministry began immediately in a couple of schools and churches. People were coming to know Jesus. We moved on to the Coromandel Peninsula for a couple more schools and churches, more people came to Jesus. We met with many families experiencing many different struggles, they came to know Jesus and victory over their personal areas of struggle. We moved south down the North Island and ministered in Wellington, Porirua, and Taita to end the trip. It was great to see God move in the lives of so many. The last church we ministered in was the Hosanna, the home church of the pastor that Shelley had met. As we were ministering there, I met Pastor Joshua, the senior pastor there and he invited me to a conference there the following weekend. That worked well for me as I was staying two extra weeks for a visit with Shelley's family.

Little did I know of the encounter the Lord had in store for me in that conference.

The conference was a prophetic conference. I was extremely interested as we had been exposed to a couple of highly gifted, anointed prophetic people in the past. Those with a prophetic gifting really seem to speak with an authority and understanding of the message of the Bible and God's plans and purposes. On the seventh of May in 1999, God spoke His plans for the future of our family very clearly.

I showed up a few minutes early to Hosanna and was treated as if I were royalty. The Maori, Samoan, and various South Pacific Islanders treat visiting pastors very respectfully. After speaking with several folks there, I was seated in a crowd of about eight hundred. When the speaker for the evening, Greg, took the stage, he hesitated for a couple of minutes, prayed and then hesitated again. This middle aged Australian man whom I had never met before, looked straight at me and said, "I need to pray for you." Quite shocked, I got up and went forward. As he prayed for me, the Lord spoke directly to me through Greg. The words were; "even though I had great faith, the Lord was calling me to make a move that far surpassed any faith that I had ever known. The Lord was going to open doors and make ways where it seemed no way was possible. This move was going to come at a strong personal cost and financial cost, that God was going to make financial provisions even as I was being prayed for." He finished by saying, "Get ready to move quickly!" Talk about a wow moment! That night as I was leaving, Joshua, the senior pastor of Hosanna invited me to meet him for lunch the next day. As I made the forty-minute ride back to Shelley's parents' home in Titahi Bay, the presence of the Lord was very thick in the car. I felt His love, His peace and His voice spoke; "I am with you." The impact of meeting Greg and hearing a very strong prophetic word spoken to me was not something a night of sleep allowed to pass.

Joshua and I met for lunch the next day as planned. God was most certainly preparing to shake our world. After a few minutes of general conversation, Joshua asked me a very big question, "How would you like to come to New Zealand and plant a church?" At that point after the night before, I was like the proverbial deer in headlights. It was all so very fast; three weeks ago, I had planned on only coming to New Zealand for a mission trip. After lunch we agreed that we would pray about the possibility of a church plant.

When I got back to the house, I called Shelley. She very quickly informed me that she had some good news to share. The rehabilitation company that she had been working for as an Occupational Therapist, offered her the regional directors job, which included a significant raise. Then it was my turn to share the news of my previous twenty- four hours. I told her about God's words to me, the increase in faith, the financial provision and a church plant. There was a silence on her end for a moment, she then replied, "if we are moving to New Zealand to plant a church, then I can't take this job." About that time God reminded me of what He had spoken about financial provision. I returned to America a couple of days later with a whole lot for us to pray about.

First thing I did when I got home was go to the mail box. there was an interesting looking letter from the Internal Revenue Service. With my legal troubles of the past, I had owed a lot of tax dollars and had not seen a tax refund in many years. I opened the envelope to a substantial refund check. If that wasn't enough, Shelley came home with the news that her company wanted her to take the direc- tor's job even if she were only there to fill it for a year. She agreed, and we agreed. We agreed to allow God to be in control of our lives totally. The time frame fell into place with the one-year job accep- tance. After that year we would move to New Zealand to plant a ministry. Now we needed to extend our faith, not just our current levels of faith, but the faith that the Holy Spirit of God would birth in us as He had spoken to me. Romans 8; 28 states, "And we know that in all things God works for the good of those who love Him, who have been called according to His purpose." We were now firmly convinced, we were called according to His purpose, He knew the plans He had for us, it was now up to us to have the faith to take the steps to see His plans for our lives become reality.

We began to prepare ourselves for the move immediately. There was so much to do as moving across the world with two young daughters would be stressful. We had a house to make arrange- ments for, personal possessions that had to be taken care of, and to prepare ourselves spiritually for the full-time ministry. The ongoing financial support had to be arranged as well.

We were trained well for the ministry in our home church. I had done some extensive leadership training through several John Maxwell seminars. I had also been through some very complete pastoral evaluations in Palm Desert and Newport Beach, California. I attended church planter's conferences and foundational Bible College training. We had no illusion that what was to come was going to be easy. Our faith was based on the fact that God was working with and for us.

God still had a couple of surprises for us.

CHAPTER 11
NOW FAITH IS

W e were really gearing up for a big year. There was a lot to plan and then also to do to move to the other side of the world. Having visited there and seeing the country, meeting Shelley's family and friends raised the excitement level for me considerably. The days were becoming weeks, the weeks turned into months, and very quickly the year ended. We had another great surprise in August 2000, we found out we were expecting another child. To add to that blessing, we found out it was to be a son. As fathers, I think we all desire to have a son, I sure did.

The plans to move were now full speed ahead. As we put all our affairs in order, I had to obtain a worker's visa to live and work in New Zealand. As a result of my criminal history, I was refused. We appealed that ruling. My appeal was to be heard at the New Zealand Embassy in Washington, DC. The scheduled date for the appeal was early April 2001. Shelley was very pregnant and was also requested to be there. We made the trip to Washington and held our breath every time we hit a bump in the road, hoping labor would not begin. Arriving in Washington and entering the Ambassador's office was a very nervous time. When we sat down, the Ambassador had my rap sheet on his desk, it looked like a small book. He asked me, while tapping on it, "Why should I allow you to live and work in New Zealand?" Shelley and I looked at each other and I responded with the only words I knew at the time, "That is a question only God can answer, it is between you and Him now." I could not believe I actually said that to this man who had the power over me moving to New Zealand and I did not know if he was even a Christian. The look he gave me in return indicated he was equally surprised with my response. After a brief conversation and my giving him the information he had asked of me, references, support plan and the associations I would have in New Zealand, the interview ended with him telling me that I would hear from him within two weeks regarding his decision.

We left Washington and made the trip home with a lot to pray for.

Less than two weeks passed, and our son was born. The level of joy over having another child and a son was another reason to celebrate God's love for us. A couple days after the birth of Eugene (Bert) Tomlinson IV we got the letter from the New Zealand Embassy informing us my application for a work visa had been approved. Praise God! We began moving at full speed ahead. We purchased my ticket to depart America May 21, 2001. Shelley and the children were booked to come over July 7, 2001. There were some arrangements still needing to be made concerning our home, possessions and Hannah finishing her year in preschool. My New Zealand in-laws were very pleased to offer us to stay with them until other plans were made. After a couple of months of planning with our church family in America and New Zealand we had a plan. The plan was to plant a church out of a café, bookstore and surf shop setting.

Before leaving America, I visited my parents on the May 20, to say our "Good-byes." It was a bit tearful. As Dad and I stood on the front porch, for what was a very emotional moment, he looked at me and spoke words that still are emotional for me, "Your grand-mother would be so very proud of you; I am so very proud of you." Dad loved and respected his mother. To hear those words from him was almost as if she was speaking them to me as well. Moma Mary was a great woman of God and had invested so much into all of our lives. I was speechless and cried. We hugged, and my relationship with my Mom and Dad had come full circle. That was the moment when I realized where God had moved me into where He was taking me.

The big day came in July for Shelley and the family to arrive. They were accompanied by our good friend and worship pastor from our home church, Mark Miller. Upon arriving in Wellington, New Zealand, I watched eagerly for my family. As they came into the airport, I was overwhelmed with joy. As I spoke, my now three-month-old son, perked right up and turned his head to my voice. The emotion of that moment overwhelmed me. Our family, together started the journey into God's plans for our lives. I once again heard God speak very clearly, "For I know the plans I have for you."

We had made some arrangements with a few churches for Mark and me to do some ministry while he was there. As we were returning from one church, we stopped and did the tourist thing on Paraparaumu Beach. After taking a couple of pictures of Kapiti Island, we turned to walk back to the car and saw this large building on a three-acre piece of land, right on the beachfront. As we both observed it, I heard a very clear voice say," That is My house, claim it." Mark was rather tall, I looked up at him and asked what he had said. He responded by saying he thought I had said it. We both heard the same thing as God spoke to us in an audible voice. I carry anointing oil with me everywhere I go. We walked up to the building and anointed doors and windows with oil and claimed the building for God. While doing this, a man came outside to see what we were doing. In the ensuing conversation, he informed us it was a community youth center. It had for many years been a pub, restaurant and hotel in the center of the beach community. As we talked we exchanged contact information. Amazed, Mark and I left.

A few days later, I got a phone call asking if I would come speak to the leaders of the same youth center. During the conversation, we were made aware it was struggling and on the verge of closing. Out of nowhere, I was asked if I would consider leading the project, with hopes it would continue to serve the community. My immediate response was yes.

The early days in New Zealand, I really experienced how much I missed home. The morning of September 12, 2001 my mother-in-law woke me with the devastating news of the terrorist attack on America. The time difference between the two countries is explanation for the date I got the news. This was terrible, and I hurt for not being around those and the country I love during this tragedy.

Within a month's time we were informed the owner of the youth center had put the property up for sale. The location was prime and many developers had eyes on it for many reasons. The real estate company contacted me and I was informed, the owner would like it to continue as a youth center and would sell it to me if I made an offer of $1.63 million. Without thinking, I said you got it. Shelley looked at me as if I were crazy. We had no money. I had ten days to raise one hundred and sixty-three thousand as a deposit. I asked anyone who would listen to no avail. On the tenth day, I met with the owner at a local café. He looked at me and said, "You don't have the money, do you?" In return, I offered to buy his coffee for him and that was the best I could do. The property was a rather prominent piece of land that had much community interest and the deal had gained interest, especially from the local newspapers. The owner, Murray, looked at me and asked; "What are we going to do about this?" Very honestly, I answered him; "This is totally up to you and God." As I was getting use to, he gave me a very bewildered look, thought for a moment and responded; "I guess we need to find a way to work this out." I had some serious work to do.

We started knocking on doors of every financial institution we could, talking to investors and trying to raise the money to purchase the property. In the meantime, Shelley was at work. She had always wanted a job that would allow her to be with our children. December and January are summer holidays in New Zealand. She devised a plan to start summer holiday programs. We had thirty some children enroll and fees were paid. We had some cash flow. We also had a café, in the building where Shelley was working, and started holding church services. This raised interest from a couple of church groups. One thing led to another and we had a church savings and development group offer us $850,000 if we would become a fellowship of a totally different denomination. This sounded a bit different, but God uses the foolish things of this world to confound the wisdom of men. We accepted their terms and were still $780,000 short. We presented what we had to the owner. He accepted our offer and informed us he would personally do a second mortgage on the balance with no interest for a year. To top it off, upon closing on the property the owner presented us with a check for $25,000. He stated to us, his partners were questioning him as they felt he did more to represent us in the purchase than he did them.

God does indeed work in mysterious ways. God reminded me of His Word once again. Hebrews 11:1 states, "Now faith is being sure of what we hope for and being certain of what we do not see." Those words; "now faith" really jumped out at me. Many times, we wait on opportunities to exercise "faith *now*." With those developments, The Kapiti Lighthouse Ministries were officially birthed.

In January 2003, we hosted a conference at The Lighthouse. We invited our prophetic friend Greg from Australia, Mark, our worship friend and several others came from America to participate in this event. At the time, we lived in a small three-bedroom house with one bathroom and a small Ford car to drive. The house was crowded and took three trips to get everyone to the revival services we were hosting, not to mention how busy the bathroom was. It was a great revival, many were saved and we baptized them in the Tasman Sea, which was just across the street. At the end of the revival, Greg felt led to pray for us again. As he prayed the Lord gave him another prophetic word for us. "The Lord has seen you and what you are doing. Prepare now for a change. The Lord has a bigger house with more rooms and bathrooms, He has more vehicles for you. This will not be your ideal house, it is the house the Lord has for you." Something about when the Lord gave us words through Greg, they could be a bit overwhelming.

At the end of the conference, I took my friend Mark back to the airport in Wellington and after saying good bye, I decided to take my friend Bill from Wilmington, NC on the scenic ride back across the Paekakeriki Hill Road, a very narrow winding road. We stopped at the top of the hill to take some great photos of the coastline and sea before continuing down. Rounding a blind curve, there coming rapidly towards us were two cars racing and one was in my lane. I had no time to react, we ran at about thirty-five miles an hour head on into one of the other cars going much faster than that. It spun my car around, threw my friend Bill from my car and I was pinned in by the steering wheel. Not really sure what happened next, my car was dangerously balanced on a berm on the side of the hill about a thousand feet straight up.

The slightest movement and my car would take a very long, surely fatal drop. When I came to, on this little travelled road, there was a truck that had appeared out of nowhere and tied a rope to the front of my car. Not sure how much time had transpired and then emergency vehicles showed up. As they were removing me from the car, I asked what was going on.

One of the emergency people, while walking me away from the car, spoke to me. When he arrived, he literally saw an angel standing at the back of my car holding it in a manner that kept it from falling off the cliff. Interestingly, no one else remembered seeing a truck with a rope attached to the front of my car either. Bill's injuries required him to be carried out by helicopter with the driver that hit us. I was taken by ambulance to the hospital in Wellington. I later found out, the emergency person speaking to me was a Christian and was convinced he saw an angel that day. Hebrews 1:14 became very real to me that day because it reads, "Are not all angels ministering spirits sent to serve those who will inherit salvation?" God reminded me, He still had plans for me and it was not for me to die on a remote, hilly road in New Zealand that day. This is a reminder to you, while reading this, that every word in the Bible is true and God so desires to reveal Himself to you in a very real way.

We continued to operate the ministry God had brought to us, no surf shop, no bookstore, a totally different plan God had. We had the children's ministry that was growing, a café that was popular and a church that grew quickly. During this first year, we struggled financially, yet we continued in faith. At the end of the year it was time to start paying on the second mortgage, that was impossible.

We met with the owner and explained our situation to him. He informed us of another property he had a couple of blocks away. It was a closed retirement home. We put our current property for sale to purchase the other property as it was more suitable to what we were doing.

The same developers that had interest previously, still had interest. We sold the property and actually made enough money to fund our new purchase. Hebrews 11:6 states, "And without faith it is impossible to please God, because anyone who comes to Him must believe that He exists and that He rewards those who earnestly seek Him." God had rewarded our faith. The new property was half the price and on six acres, forty-five rooms of accommodation, five self-contained apartments and a large kitchen and meeting room. This was the larger house with more bedrooms and bathrooms and no it was not the ideal in our opinion.

God had plans to expand our ministry. We went from one small car to a van and, then to four vans. We went from wondering if we would continue our children's programs, to reaching our maximum of eighty very quickly. With our rooms, we started providing emergency housing for many people with many various needs, we had The Kapiti Foodbank, Kapiti Toy Lending library and the local Meals on Wheels on our property. God had definitely brought many needs meeting ministries to us.

Right across the street from us was a motorcycle shop. There was a social club that also met there. God was getting ready to expand our family and ministry again. In 2003, we gave birth to our first New Zealand born child, Grace Margaret. That word "Grace" was a constant reminder to us. John 3:16, "For God so loved the world that He gave His one and only Son, that whoever believes in Him shall not perish but have eternal life."

God was bringing a lot of "Who-evers" around us. We did not get it perfect all the time, but we did try. We learned many lessons the hard way, yet God was still faithful. When we first moved to New Zealand, our plan was three to five years. God was adjusting that plan and our vision at that time was to be there as long as God desired. Bert was now four years old and had a love for anything with two wheels and a gasoline engine. We went down to the motor cycle shop and found a great bike for him, on the way out the door, there was a pretty, black, Harley Davidson Sportster for sale. It was impulsive and totally out of the blue, but I spoke to Shelley and she liked the idea. Within a couple of days, I added biker to the list of many other personal descriptions. As it happened, I was asked to join the club. The conditions the club placed on me were, they knew I was a pastor, I could not preach to them, but if questions were asked of me, I could answer them. I started getting many questions about my beliefs and being a Christian. Many of the people in the group found a level of happiness in the association with each other as it represented family to them. We had a desire for them to find happiness in God. As the church was growing, the ministry became very successful. We saw many come to a saving knowledge of Jesus Christ and we baptized many. We saw many people healed and set free from their bondages of sin in their lives. We enjoyed serving the Lord and we trusted God's leadership in our lives.

The new property that we were on bordered the airport in Paraparaumu. This airport had a pilot training school. We were approached about housing the students of that school and agreed to do that. Very quickly we had several international students move in with us. Most of the students came from India. Over the course of the next couple of years we learned a lot about Indian culture, we ate a lot of curries. These students had many different beliefs, India is the land of a million gods. As with any other type of schooling, these students had tests. They knew I was a Christian, and a pastor, which led to many conversations about our different spiritual beliefs. Some of the students were Hindu, Buddhists, and some were Christian. The first time they had a test, a couple of the Christian students asked me to pray for them to be successful in the test. At that point there were about twenty of them. The two that I prayed for passed the test and the rest had to take the test over. On the day scheduled for the second test, I heard a knock on my door and there was a line of students there asking me to pray for each of them to pass. I had to chuckle a bit. They all passed that time and it became the norm for me to have prayer time with each of them before their tests.

In early 2004, we learned that we were expecting another child. In October we welcomed Elizabeth Joyce into our family. We were now a family with five children and felt very blessed with all God had brought around us.

The Lord was really faithful to us during these years. He kept bringing so many people around us. Our children's programs grew and grew. We built a new building to house a new youth center and were able to put the food bank in a larger home. Most of the people that God was bringing to us had very high levels of need and we learned there was a big difference in preaching to people and ministering in a manner that met their very real needs. Our perception of church was changing, it wasn't only how good a sermon you could preach, it was also loving on people in a very real way.

I had grown to really enjoy my Harley time and the friendships I had formed riding with so many of the guys. The country of New Zealand is so very beautiful from Cape Reinga on the top of the North Island to Invercargill on the bottom of the South Island. It did not take much to encourage me to take off for a week and go for a ride. I traded my Sportster for a 2002 Night Train and loved it.

Shelley had a staff of probably twenty to help with the children's programs. We had before school care that started at 6:30 in the morning, we fed them breakfast and then took them to school. We had after-school care, where we picked up children from seven local schools and kept them busy doing homework, crafts and sporting activities until their parents picked them up. We also had school holiday programs. The school schedule for New Zealand was ten weeks of class and then two weeks off. This was the consistent schedule year-round. We were very busy, living there on a remodeled part of the property that housed our family.

For me personally, life was good. I had a wife, a family and a home. God brought us to a great place in ministry. We learned so very much about God's love to us, for us and saw how He loved so many others. We did experience some very tough and trying times. I had several of my biking friends die and performed their funerals. There were others for whom I performed marriage ceremonies.

With Elizabeth being a baby and our family needing a break, we decided to take a trip to Australia in November of 2004. It had been a very long and busy three years. As we flew into Brisbane Airport a reminder of my past popped up. Upon going through customs, I was separated from my family by the officials. I was taken into a holding area and interviewed for about an hour as to why I was in Australia. When they checked my passport, it was flagged due to my criminal past with drugs. With my young family in a bit of shock we waited to see if they were going to turn me away, thankfully they didn't. We enjoyed our break there. I think God just wanted to show me the life He had separated me from that I would never go back to.

Psalms 103:11-12 states, "For as high as the heavens are above the earth, so great is His love for those who fear Him; as far as the east is from the west, so far has He removed our transgressions from us."

What a great reminder of how God works with and for us. He literally moved me to the other side of the world to remove me from my sins.

The next couple of years had some real highs and lows. Shelley's parents joined us in our ministry. They helped in so many valuable areas. We now had six vans, Shelley's Dad drove one of them to drop children at school, pick them up from school and take them where they needed to go in the afternoons, including music lessons, sporting events, etc. We had Children's Church on Sunday mornings for children only, this was called" Hop on the Bus". Shelley's Dad would pick them up from their homes and take them back. Shelley's mom was the best administrative person we could have ever wished for.

I stayed busy in ministry. I helped a small church about thirty-minute drive away many Sundays, we had our services on Sunday evenings. We continued to see the positive change in many lives as we ministered the Love of God through the life of His Son Jesus. God continued to bless us as our family was growing up. Our children were so great to share their mom with eighty some children every day from 630 am till 630 pm. We even had a couple of children move in with us who became just like family.

Life began to change for us in 2006. My mother had been battling cancer for several years. I got a phone call that Mom was going to Duke Medical for some treatment, this treatment was to help her get better and she would be in the hospital for a week or so. I made arrangements to go home and be with Dad while she was away. Upon landing at the airport, my brother picked me up and very sadly told me my mother had passed away the day before.

While I was home, I spoke at several local churches and began to sense maybe God was calling us back. Returning to New Zealand was tough. It was clear though that the work God had called us to was not yet done there. There was the feeling we had to finish well. Over the next few years God kept us very busy. Our children's programs were recognized by the government of New Zealand as the best in the country for our work with children and families from 2006 through 2012. An honor many found amazing, as we were told the government was hesitant to recognize Christian ministries in that manner. There were 1,300 other such programs in the country. Such an honor for Shelley and the staff, they all worked so very hard.

My life stayed the same, I rode my Harley a lot, enjoyed relationships with guys that you would never imagine would speak about the Lord. In all reality, I was sensing there was more for me. I wasn't sure what it was, I was sure however, that change was coming. I was praying one day and the Lord gave me the scripture Isaiah 43:18-19, "Forget the former things, do not dwell on the past. See, I am doing a new thing! Now it springs up; do you not perceive it? I am making a way in the desert and streams in the wasteland."

I was beginning to perceive the changes, and was looking for the way God was going to make.

CHAPTER 12
GOD MADE THE WAY

The next several years we were doing what we felt God had called us to. For me, personally, I was a bit bored. I was filling my life with a lot of activities and staying busy, yet I was uneasy desiring more. Yes, living to serve God was great; there were challenges. It seemed like life had gotten a bit too predictable. With my past being so filled with challenges, it seemed I needed a new thing to challenge me. Since my mother had passed, my father started battling dementia. As a family, we visited America in 2009 and then again in 2012. The children really enjoyed their time with their Granddad and seeing America. It was during those visits that I started dreaming of moving home. The question was, how?

In early February 2013, I got a call from family that Dad was entering his last days. I got a plane ticket home immediately. I got home in time to spend some time with him before he passed away on the morning of the February 13. This was a bitter sweet time. Shelley with Hannah, Kaely and Bert came over for the funeral. At that time, we all began to sense the change coming. All my life I had a desire to move back to Southport with the ambition of planting a church. During our time at home I met with several representatives of The North Carolina Baptist State Convention. By God's timing only, a Baptist church planting conference was being held a week after Dad's funeral and they invited me to attend. The morning I was leaving Southport, to go to Camp Caraway outside of Asheboro, N.C. for the week, I was just really confused as to what was going on. Getting in the car, listening to Christian Radio the Lord spoke directly to me. First thing I heard was a story about a pilot awaiting take-off and it being stalled as there were clouds that would hinder it. Secondly, their scripture passage for the day that came from Joshua 1:9 stating, "Have I not commanded you? Be strong and courageous. Do not be terrified, do not be discouraged, for the Lord your God will be with you wherever you go." If that wasn't enough, a popular song, *It's Only a Mountain*, came on. Three very direct encouragements to me from the Lord. The scripture, Matthew 17:20 immediately came to mind, "He replied, because you have so little faith, I tell you the truth, if you have faith as small as a mustard seed, you can say to this mountain, 'Move' from here to there and it will move. Nothing will be impossible for you."

I heard the Lord speaking directly to me. The conference was great, it was a week to refresh and focus on moving out in the Lord. I returned to my family and then New Zealand the following week.

Two weeks after returning, early on a Saturday morning, Shelley's dad suffered a stroke and passed away. We lost both our fathers in the span of a month. We were saddened by this and left wondering what was next.

The year of 2013 flew by. In August, I attended a conference at which my friend Greg was speaking in Hamilton, New Zealand. This was a very prophetic conference and the presence of the Lord was very evident in the meetings. During the last night of the meetings, during a time of worship, the Lord had me on my knees seeking more of Him. In that moment, He had me open my Bible and it opened directly to Ezekiel 43:1-2, "Then the man brought me to the gate facing east, and I saw the Glory of the God of Israel coming from the east. His voice was like the roar of rushing waters and the land was radiant with His Glory."

Immediately I knew the Lord was speaking to me. It was time to move home. In my spirit, the gate facing east represented the Cape Fear River and Southport. Greg came to me and wanted to pray for me immediately after this. The words he spoke were so confirming. He said, "This is not for you to understand, this is by faith, you will move and the Lord will move you and provide for you to make this move." Something about Greg praying for me over the years, God always did what Greg was obedient to speak to me. I left the conference and went out to Raglan, it was a forty-five-minute ride. While there, at the same motel God spoke to me fifteen years earlier, He confirmed to me, my days were coming to an end in New Zealand.

Upon returning to Paraparaumu, I received the news the tenants in our home in Wilmington, NC had moved out and the house needed a lot of work. I was back off to America to prepare our house for more tenants. There was so much work to do, painting the exterior, rebuilding our screened in porch, our yard was a wreck, I mean a lot of work had to be done. My return ticket to New Zealand was for November 17, 2017. The work in New Zealand was moving forward as we were surrounded with good staff and those very capable of filling my shoes, we had been working in New Zealand twelve years at that point. On November 15, I got a call from our realtor as we had now listed our home in Wilmington to sell. He explained that our house needed the entire interior painted.

There I was, supposed to leave two days later, how could I accomplish that feat? About three hours later, I got a call from a member of the interim pastor search committee at Southport Baptist Church asking if I would be available to speak the following Sunday for three services. At the time, the church was in transition as the Senior Pastor had moved. I spoke with Shelley and we extended my plane ticket for ten days. It was a very interesting week, as my days were very busy painting and my nights were full of time worshipping and seeking the Lord. Sunday came, and I spoke at the two morning services. It was a great blessing to speak in the church I grew up in and was baptized in early in my life. I went back to speak at the evening service. A dear lady, that had known me all my life came to me at the end of that service and said to me, "Son this is where you belong, come home now." She looked me in the eyes as she said this and I knew it was real. As I left that evening, I left my resume with the interim pastor search committee.

Upon my return to New Zealand, I told Shelley we were moving back. Quite startled, she agreed it was time. We had both been sensing the "new thing" God was going to do. As Shelley and I spoke, we were aware of the magnitude of the move, not only for us, but for our now five children as well. We were moving them all from everything they knew, their friends, school, activities, it was major. When Shelley asked how we would do this, I said we had to sell my Harley, the property in New Zealand and our house in Wilmington. We spent a quick month with family and friends making arrangements to move back to America. We did not know how it would happen or what it would look like, but God did. On December 31, 2013, I boarded an airplane once again for America, this time with a one-way ticket. The week after I arrived in Wilmington, Shelley called to tell me a man was there with cash to purchase my Harley, we agreed to the price. The price was enough to purchase the plane tickets and a shipping container to bring our possessions to America. Shelley and the children came to America on January 21, 2014. We still were trusting God for provision. In the middle of February 2014, we got a call from our realtor in New Zealand informing us we had a full price offer on our property. The confirming aspect of this was, the people buying had agreed to continue our ministry there. To top it off, they also agreed to pay Shelley a year's salary to continue to consult for the children's programs, over the phone and via e-mail. We had a considerable financial interest in the property we had now owned for twelve years. The last day of March 2014 the deal closed, God's provision for our move was realized.

When we first arrived back, our children wanted to live on the beach. It was winter time and the rental homes on Long Beach had great rates. We found one on Long Beach with five bedrooms, fully furnished, right across the street from the ocean. God was so faithful. The testimony to His faithfulness, we had to move in order for Him to reward our faith. We had indeed heard from Him.

Our faith was stretched during the next six months, we still neither had jobs. The children were in school, adjusting was a test for them, but they all did very well.

In the meantime, our family home was still vacant since my father's passing, we felt that was meant to be our home. We purchased the house from the other members of the family and moved back into the home I grew up in, right across the street from my most favorite place in the world, The Cape Fear River. We made some additions to the home, each child had their own bedroom and they were happy.

Southport Baptist Church was still without a pastor, I continued to preach a couple of Sundays a month. During that time, their worship pastor and youth pastor were called to other churches as well. The search committee brought several candidates before the church and they just weren't able to hire them. God was now speaking clearly to Shelley and me, "This is where you will be."

After meeting with the interim committee and being told they were not going to call me, we stood, trusting God. Three days after the interim committee told me I would not be a candidate, the Senior Pastor search committee called me and wanted to meet with me. They informed me that they had some three hundred applications for the job and mine had been in the "No" pile during their search. They further explained that by some strange reason, every time they studied the resumes, mine kept falling out in front of them. Then the question came, "Are you still interested in being the Senior Pastor of Southport Baptist Church?"

Shelley and I were overcome with joy in that moment. We knew God had plans. We had a great meeting and it ended with the encouragement, they may call again. A week later they did call again. They asked if we knew what we were there for? Very boldly I answered, "You are getting ready to offer me a job."

I think my response stunned them as they had agreed no one would speak about it. Then they confirmed, yes, they were offering me the job. August 2, 2014, I preached the morning service, after which, the church voted to hire me as the Senior Pastor.

I was back to the town I grew up in, to the home I grew up in, to the church I grew up in. God truly did take my life full circle. He alone is faithful. Jesus speaks personally to each person, Matthew

19: 26 states, "Jesus replied, 'With man this is impossible, but with God all things are possible!'" It's time to allow your hope, your dreams, and your fantasies to become realities with God. May God bless you all.

IN CONCLUSION

We have been home just over four years now. I have been the Pastor for three years. Shelley is doing what she loves, caring for people as an Occupational Therapist. Hannah is now almost twenty-two, a rising senior in college. Kaely is now nineteen and a sophomore in college. Bert is sixteen and all boy: he loves hunting, fishing, surfing, sports and anything that does not interfere with them. Grace is fourteen and seems inclined to pursue the hopes of owning her own restaurant or becoming a doctor. Elizabeth is our twelve-year-old baby, and such a gift. God is so good when we move into those places He can truly bless. I have the wife, home, and family I prayed for so many years ago.

Writing this book has been quite a journey for me. I in no way want to glamorize myself through the flame years. I am sure we can all experience them. The reality, no matter the heat of the flames, the cross of Jesus is our redemption through His grace poured out for us each. The inspiration to write was a God thing for me to share at this time as well. While attending a pastor's conference in Orlando,

Florida in November of 2016, I met representatives of Xulon Press. We talked a few times and my interest was stirred by them.

On the evening of November 28, 2016, I had an outdoor fire in our backyard. As I was relaxing by the fire, the Lord spoke to me, "Take a picture of the fire." The Lord knows I love to take pictures, but I asked," Why?" His response was; "Take the picture and you will see! "I did not see what He wanted me to take a picture of. After taking the picture, I went to my pictures and saw a cross rising out of the flames. The Lord spoke, "There is the cover to your book and there in it is the title." That is how I decided to name my book, *Through the Flames to the Cross*.

The writing started in January of this year and has been a wonderful experience. The way to make this more wonderful is for it to speak to you in a manner that it brings His plans for you to become a reality in your life.

I would like for you to ask yourselves the following questions after reading this book.

Have you ever seriously pursued the knowledge of the plans God has for your life?

What does the message of Jesus being more than Savior but also Lord of your life mean to you?

We all have our own levels of faith, what does the definition faith mean to you? "Now Faith" what does this mean?

Do you believe that God can speak to you through others you do not even know?

CONCERNING PROPHECY

2 Peter 1:19-21 states, "And we have the word of the prophets made more certain, and you will do well to pay attention to it, as to a light shining in a dark place, until the day dawns and the morning start rises in your hearts. Above all, you must understand that no prophecy of scripture came about by the prophet's own interpretation. For prophecy never had its origin in the will of man, but men spoke from God as they were carried along by the Holy Spirit."

CPSIA information can be obtained
at www.ICGtesting.com
Printed in the USA
FSHW04n2201030318
45263FS